PRAISE FOR
WOUNDED BY TRUTH —
HEALED BY LOVE

With profound simplicity, David Cartwright brings thoughtful and provocative exegesis to what at first glance seem to be contradictory teachings of Jesus. He provides keen insight into the biblical, cultural, and religious context of Jesus' "uncommon sense" for important questions and issues of his time - and ours. This book is loaded with concreteness and specificity as Cartwright examines both the then and the now.

The author fills the chapters with pertinent illustrations, many from his own life experiences. He is unafraid to allow his humanity to show as he deals with many "on the one hand, but on the other hand" paradoxical situations. It is evident that in his reflections Cartwright has done the hard work of clarifying perplexing and seemingly conflicting biblical texts. In so doing, he has given us the basics we need to discover some of Jesus' healing truths for these critical times.

Ronald Higdon
Retired seminary professor, intentional interim specialist and certified church consultant and facilitator, author of
Surviving a Son's Suicide

David Cartwright's book *Wounded by Truth and Healed by Love* is a careful and thought-provoking study of several of the paradoxical teachings of Jesus. Cartwright does not offer easy answers to what appear to be contradictory sayings of Jesus but provides an honest struggle to discern the meaning of selected controversial texts. He draws upon current scholarship but states clearly his own appraisal or apparent conclusion after wrestling with the texts. His personal stories, excerpts from literature and other illustrations enliven and clarify his interpretation of the meaning of the texts for today. The sermons in this book offer a good model on how one can preach on some of the difficult and what appear to be contradictory sayings of Jesus.

William Powell Tuck
Interim Pastor of Westover Baptist Church, Richmond, VA,
and author of several books including
Overcoming Sermon Block: The Preacher's Workshop

Open the Gospels to the words and works of Jesus, and it doesn't take long before you encounter two of his teachings that are at odds with one another. Or are they? *Wounded by Truth – Healed by Love* embraces the paradoxical teachings of Jesus. David Cartwright skillfully handles these seemingly contradictory truths as if they were each part of a beautiful tapestry: carefully crafted and woven into a beautiful pattern. And yet the Word of God is just that – a collection of thoughts and ideas beautifully woven into a larger story.

Which of us hasn't wrestled with contradictory statements and felt less than satisfied with our conclusions? Were it not for my belief in the inspiration of the Holy Spirit upon the pages of Scripture, I might be forced to conclude that the Jesus' own words were at odds with one another. That David Cartwright has confidently handled Scripture for many years is evident in this book. *Wounded by Truth – Healed by Love* is one of the finest approaches to difficult biblical passages that I've read in a long time.

Christopher Bozung, D. Min
author of *Uncommon Questions from an Extraordinary Savior*

David Cartwright admits the truth about Christianity today and how we have forgotten that the aroma that God desires is that of humility and love. We are human with all the glorious flaws and fears and failures that come along with us. The truth can hurt but it also heals when accompanied by love because love never fails. Cartwright reminds us of this truth and provides a call to action for Christians everywhere – remember to love. I would also add that he provides beautiful images of service and humility that are inspiring. He reminds us that service is love with boots on – not crowns!

Shauna Hyde
Pastor of Ravenswood UMC and author of *Fifty Shades of Grace*

David Cartwright provides a great service to the Church. With a seasoned pastor's skill, a theologian's heart, and the experience of a Christian who has long struggled with these issues, the author gives us real, meaningful ways to look at those times in Holy Writ where there are paradoxes. The example he provides is that of someone who loves Scripture and wishes to call more people to struggle with it.

Joel Watts, UnsettledChristianity.com
Editor of *From Fear to Faith*.

WOUNDED BY TRUTH

—

HEALED BY LOVE

REFLECTIONS ON THE PARADOXICAL TEACHINGS OF JESUS

DAVID R. CARTWRIGHT

Energion Publications
Gonzalez, FL
2014

ISBN10: 1-63199-117-5
ISBN13: 978-1-63199-117-2
Library of Congress Control Number: 2014957898

Energion Publications
P. O. Box 841
Gonzalez, FL 32560

energion.com
pubs@energion.com
850-525-3916

TABLE OF CONTENTS

DEDICATION

To Christopher and Megan

who practice what their father tries to preach

Lord, your word is sharper than any two-edged sword,
piercing both heart and conscience with many wounds.
May the wounds that are made by your truth
be healed by your love. Amen.
(A traditional prayer for illumination)

PREFACE

I have been fascinated with some of the teachings of Jesus for almost as long as I can remember. It must have been when I was in elementary school that my ears perked up when I realized that one Sunday my minister quoted Jesus as saying, "He who is not against us is for us," and then not long after that, "He who is not for us is against us." These two sayings of Jesus set me on what has turned out to be a life-long quest to understand what I often refer to as "the paradoxical teachings of Jesus." I confess that, at times, my fascination has also become frustration, if not outright bewilderment. The fifteen chapters in this little volume are the result of my own personal attempt to make sense out of what often seemed to me that Jesus was speaking out of both sides of his mouth at once. Now I have come to look upon these teachings of Jesus as "complimentary opposites," in the best sense of those words.

To set the record straight, I do not in any way claim to be a New Testament scholar. Hopefully, I am an informed pastor and preacher, one who takes seriously the need to grapple with the hard passages of scripture as well as the more easily accessible, even more likable ones. Though not versed in Greek, in my study of these teachings of Jesus, I have tried to consult the best commentaries in English I could lay my hands on.

Also, I am aware of the continuing debate about the Jesus Seminar. While I am aware of some of their conclusions, personally I have to say that I agree with some of the results and disagree with others. I also have a lingering hesitancy to sign off completely on the underlying methodology as well. But with that said, for me, the question, "What would Jesus do?" goes back to a more basic one,

"What did Jesus mean?" And with that question, further back to an even more basic one, "What did Jesus say?" What I can claim to have discerned from all this discussion is that it has made me dive deeper into my study of the New Testament, and at the same time gain a deeper appreciation for the variety and diversity of its authors. I am primarily a "Sunday-in and Sunday-out" preacher; I have an ongoing commitment to the Canon as it has been preserved and transmitted to us. While there may be many different sound teachings, there is finally only one Jesus who said them.

I am convinced that there are no easy answers. I constantly find myself thinking, "it all depends," a phrase which the reader will see appears again and again in what follows. I guess the main lesson I have received to date is that whatever Jesus said, he never meant it to be used as an excuse for letting ourselves off the hook.

I want to express my gratitude to several individuals who have been so helpful to me over the last three years, as I tried to pull all this together and put it into a readable, if not memorable form. First, to my wife, Susan, who is my best compassionate critic, as well as computer "tech." Without her help, these words would never have seen the light of day. And to the congregation of Hazelwood Christian Church (Disciples of Christ) in Muncie, Indiana where I delivered many, but not all, of these sermons during my ministry there. Their encouragement was invaluable, not to speak of the precious gift of a sabbatical time for reflection. Then to the Lilly Endowment, Inc. for the generous Clergy Renewal Grant which allowed me and my family to spend several weeks during the 2004 Easter Term at Wesley House in Cambridge, England where I did much of the basic research for these scriptures. (Which also explains why there are far too many illustrations from this delightful period in my life. Like any preacher knows, if I could have found better examples than these, I would have used them.) It goes without saying, that any limitations these messages have are totally and completely mine.

Finally, my prayer is that all who read these words will ultimately find themselves confronted not with what I have to say, but with the Jesus who originally said them.

David Cartwright
Muncie, Indiana
Season of Pentecost, 2014

CHAPTER 1

A TWO-EDGED SWORD

Luke 10:1-12, Luke 22:24-27, Luke 35-38

Jesus taught in paradoxes. Some of these are obvious. The first shall be last. Those who lose their lives will find it. Humble yourself and you will be exalted. Other of Jesus' teachings are more subtle, and harder to detect. These teachings can be seen when a certain saying is compared with another, such as we see in the scriptures from Luke, Chapters 10 and 22. Either way, obvious or subtle, outright or hidden, Jesus taught paradoxically. Perhaps an even better way to describe how he went about it might be to call his teachings - complimentary opposites.

Now, a paradox occurs when two truths that seem contradictory on the surface are viewed from a larger perspective and actually turn out to be parts of a greater truth. That is, a paradox is when two apparently contradictory truths *converge* into one larger, over-arching truth. For example, when cars were first introduced, many horse and buggy operations went out of business. They could not see the bigger picture. They didn't know that they were in the transportation business. For those that did realize this, they were able to make the transition. Some in a big way. Many of Jesus' sayings turn out to be like this. Many of Jesus' teachings in themselves point to a larger truth above the partial truths. But it takes eyes to see and ears to hear to discern this, as he said on more than one occasion.

The two passages from Luke, Chapter 10 and 22 are classic examples of paradoxical teachings. I chose these initially because they are among the more readily accessible. The first teaching in Luke10 comes from Jesus' early ministry. Jesus has already commissioned the twelve to serve as his disciples. Now he extends the number to 70 or 72. Not all texts agree on the number. Seventy is the more likely, since it's a symbolic number. For instance, the Bible tells us that there were 70 elders who assisted Moses and 70 offspring of Jacob. The reason the number of disciples needs to be enlarged is because the job is getting bigger. "The harvest is plentiful, but the laborers are few ..."

Jesus then sends the seventy out with these instructions: "I am sending you out like lambs into the midst of wolves. Carry no purse, no bag, no sandals, and greet no one on the road." And so on. These seventy are utterly to rely on God for everything they need. Whatever they need, God will provide it for them. They can count on that.

The setting for the second scripture is Luke Chapter 22. It takes place during the Last Supper. Rather than at the beginning of Jesus' ministry, this scripture occurs shortly before the end. Right in the middle of the Passover meal, we see that the disciples are jockeying for power. Luke tells us, "A dispute also arose among them as to which one of them was to be regarded as the greatest." Jesus sets them straight. The kingdom of God does not work this way. In the world, you have those in authority. They are called benefactors. "But not so with you; rather the greatest among you must become like the youngest, and the leader like the one who serves."

After setting them straight about these matters, Jesus tells Peter that he (Peter) will let him down in the crisis that's impending. Peter denies it vehemently. And it's here we find our next teaching. It's traditionally known as the Two Swords. Jesus says, "When I sent you out without a purse, bag or sandals, did you lack anything?" They said, "No, not a thing. " He said to them, "But now, the one who has a purse must take it, and likewise a bag. And the one who has no sword must sell his cloak and buy one." Picking up on the need for a sword, the disciples say, "Lord, look, here are two swords." Jesus replied, "It is enough."

And with these words, the controversy begins. Purse, no purse; bag, no bag; coat, no coat; sandals, no sandals; Sword, no sword. Which is it? It all depends, it seems.

Though open to many ways of interpretation, this is how I interpret these scriptures. The larger truth to which they point is the question: "What is fitting?" The concern is what is needed now, in this specific situation. As I read these verses in Luke 22, the time has come to update, even correct, the original instructions given in Luke 10. The early instructions Jesus gave to his disciples were applicable, given the conditions of the ministry at that time. Now they no longer apply. The situation has changed. New measures are required.

Does Jesus really mean it when he says now it's time to sell their cloaks and purchase a sword? Some commentators say he does. Others say no. Some say Jesus is speaking symbolically here. Either way, the problem is that the disciples just don't get it. It's another of those times when they don't comprehend what their teacher is trying to tell them.

I think the over-arching truth these scriptures are pointing to is the same truth as the Boy Scout Motto: "Be prepared." In the beginning, it was ok, maybe even helpful, for the disciples to travel light. No purse, no bag, no sandals. That was how they needed to prepare for the mission. Now, things have changed, and dramatically. Hostility toward Jesus and his mission is rising. Stronger measures are required. Purse, bag, sandals are necessary now. And now to carry a sword is not only ok, but maybe even necessary, given this stage in the ministry.

One thing we know for sure is that some of the disciples already had a sword with them. In fact, Luke says there were two swords readily available at the Last Supper.

When Jesus learns of these two swords, he says, "It is enough." What does he mean? Does he mean that two swords are more than they need? Is that it? Some commentators say no. This is not what Jesus means at all. Others take a slightly different tack. They say that when Jesus saw that even his disciples were carrying swords, his heart was broken. They still hadn't gotten his message of nonviolence. It's like a mother's disappointment in her children. When they're acting up, she can't keep from shaking her head and saying, "I can't seem to do a thing with them." Still others say that Jesus is acknowledging that there is no way around violence in this world. It's bound to happen. "It is enough" means "Let them have their way." And sadly, even his disciples will be a part of it.

How we interpret these passages is not just a matter for scholars to debate *ad infinitum*. The Two Sword passage has been used by some Christians to justify going to war and by others to justify having nothing to do with it. As for myself, I'm not a pacifist, but neither am I a war hawk. I like to think I'm a Christian realist. So I can see how these scriptures might apply both to situations of war and nonviolence. Taken together with other things Jesus had to say, it helps me see what the other side is talking about. At the very least, by looking intently at scriptures such as these in Luke 10 and 22, we should not rush too quickly to an assessment.

This is about as far as I'm willing to go. Taken together, these two passages from Luke force us to ask the right questions. They do not necessarily give us the answers we're looking for. But they do point us to the right questions. It's up to us to make the hard decisions.

Take an example from my childhood. Actually, it could be from any boy's childhood. That is, any boy who knew a little about the teachings of Jesus. As I was growing up, the Christian faith could be tough on a little guy. When confronted with what seems to be called for, to bloody your best friend's nose, many a Christian little boy hears Jesus' words in the tones of his mother's whisper, "If one strikes you on the cheek, turn the other to him also." At the time, the choice feels something like this: "Fight like a man or be a Christian like Jesus." At least that's the way it's has been presented to many little Christian boys. And that puts those little Christian boys, and girls for that matter, in a terrible dilemma. How can they ever survive and grow up, let alone live as God and their parents want them to? I'm sure that many little boys and girls give up trying to figure it out.

And to make matters worse, things don't get much better the older we get. By the time we're adolescents, many young men and women have given up on trying to live in the real world and be a Christian at the same time. When faced with how to behave when out with the guys, more than one well-meaning young man or woman has decided that if there are seven deadly sins close at hand, there also must be seven deadly virtues nearby as well. We may not even need the words of the musical, *Camelot*, to rhyme them for us, but here they are nonetheless: "Fie on goodness fie. It's not the earth the meek inherit, it's the dirt." For many a young man and woman, living in the real world and following the commandments of God are just incompatible. Like Demas in the New Testament, they pass into the ranks of those who once loved Christ, but have now gone after other things.

This is not only a problem for little boys and young adolescents. From the looks of things over the last few years, it seems to be getting harder and harder every day to stay honest and make a go of it in "the real world." It has probably never been easy, but there did seem to be a time when some in business were dedicated to "good Christian principles." I'm not saying there aren't good Christian businesses still around these days. Indeed, in some places, there are evidences of individuals and firms that go out of their way to conduct their work in a manner that Jesus would approve. What I am saying is that it seems to be getting harder and harder to pull it off. The reason is this. There doesn't seem to be as much support from the general culture as there once was. For instance, there once was a time when it was good for business to be in church; now no one seems to care where you are on Sunday morning.

What kind of life did Jesus intend for us? Do you have to be a sucker to be a Christian? If you follow the Lord, will you end up being a doormat for others to wipe their feet on? If so, is it any wonder that many young people part company with the Christian faith as quickly as possible? Even the mere appearance of this kind of Christianity is enough to make them head for the nearest exit.

The tragedy is that too often they part company with Jesus just at the time they may need him most. And even more tragic is that they may reject Jesus and his teachings before they've even had the opportunity to find out what they are. At these times, what's rejected is a caricature of the Christian religion, not the real thing itself. What's rejected is a one-sided view of the gospel. Not knowing the real Jesus, and not being able to live according to the Jesus they do know, many young people are literally forced to reject Jesus before they've even accepted him. Sadly, what they reject should be rejected. What's even sadder is that what they could have accepted was never ever presented to them.

This need never happen if the church were more careful in how it presents Jesus. As one has put it, "We have no right to be more Christian than Christ was." And yet this is so often what seems to happen in the church. We present a Jesus to our youth, and to ourselves, that's more Christian than Jesus ever was. We present a one-sided, cardboard Jesus. When in actuality, the real Jesus is sharper than any two-edged sword. The Jesus who attracts me is no department store mannequin, but a living, breathing human being who sweats out the decisions of life, such as whether to fight or turn the other cheek. The Jesus who attracts me and demands my loyalty is the one who says "Carry no purse, no bag, and no sandals." And then later, "But now, the one who has a purse must take it, and likewise a bag. And the one who has no sword must sell his cloak and buy one." That's the Jesus who fascinates and frustrates me, the idealist and the realist all wrapped up into one. That's an offer I cannot turn down. For that's a Jesus who knows what life's about on all accounts.

Would that every little boy were taught all the words of Jesus as well as the more familiar ones. Would that every adolescent knew the whole Christian story when making decisions that will affect the rest of their lives. Would that every person in business had them engraved on the back of their desk plates so they could see them every day.

Recently in America there is a revival of the musical, *Fiddler on the Roof.* It is once again playing to standing room only crowds and receiving rave reviews. One of my favorite scenes is the opening prologue. When the musical drama opens, a middle age Jewish man is playing a fiddle while he's standing precariously on a steep roof top. As the enchanting music continues in the background, we hear these words, "A fiddler on the roof; sounds crazy, no? But in our little village of Anatevka you might say, that each one of us is a fiddler on the roof, trying to scratch out a pleasant simple tune without breaking his neck." That's not only the problem of the Russian Jew of days gone by; it's the problem of those of us who are trying to be a Christian every day. How do you scratch out a pleasant simple tune in this life without breaking your neck? How do you fiddle on the roof without losing your balance? That's the question.

For the Fiddler, there's only one way. And that is Tradition with a capital T. To hold to tradition when everything's changing, that's the answer. For some Christians, that also seems to be the only way. But for others of us, there is another way. And that is to follow the advice of Jesus. But his way is actually a sword that cuts two ways. Purse, no purse; bag, no bag; sandals, no sandals; sword, no sword? It all depends. So when faced with these kinds of decisions, the least that we should do is to stop and think a little longer before we take action. Because it's right here that Jesus leaves us on our own. And although it may not feel like it, this is one of those times when it is to our advantage that he goes away.

You see, Jesus refuses to make our decisions for us. Instead, he gives us a method to make our decisions. He gives us a way to go about making them. That's part of what it means to me when he says "I am the way." He does not tell me exactly what to do. I have to decide that.

So it is also with the Bible as a whole. In my way of understanding, the Bible is a guide book. It's not a prescription book with a list for each and every case. In some ways, the Bible is more like a do-it-yourself book. Yes, the instructions are there about how to make a temple. But you, and only you, have to figure what to do if the board you are using has a knothole in it. Jesus knew that. That's why we hear him say over and over again, "Those with ears to hear, listen."

CHAPTER 2
TO SPEAK OR NOT TO SPEAK?

Mark 1:40-45, Mark 5:18-20, Mark 8:27-30, Mark 9:9-10, Mark 14:60-68

Jesus arrived on the scene proclaiming the coming of the Kingdom of God. To listen to Jesus tell it, the Kingdom was a place of all-inclusive grace where everyone could find a welcome. This was his message. And preaching this message was his heartfelt passion. He never tired of telling stories about what the Kingdom was like.

Why, then, did he tell some people to spread the good news of the Kingdom and others to keep quiet about it? Why this seeming contradictory way of going about it? Jesus' method of spreading the message was as paradoxical as the message itself. How come? And more importantly, could it be that if we can decipher the reason (or reasons) Jesus did this, we might also discover how to deal with those times when we are faced with the dilemma of deciding whether to speak or remain silent?

Four scenes, vignettes, if you will, from Mark's Gospel show us four times when Jesus is called upon to decide whether to speak out or to keep silent. These four occasions can assist us in arriving at an answer about how Jesus went about making a decision.

The first scene is in the very first chapter of Mark's gospel. A leper comes to Jesus begging to be healed. He knows that Jesus can heal him if he will. Mark tells us that Jesus was moved with pity and reached out to the man and said, "I do choose. Be made clean." And immediately the man's leprosy went away.

Just what disease the man had is not all that clear. The Biblical disease of leprosy is not always to be identified with the modern day disease by that name. The Bible word for leprosy seems to cover many different kinds of skin ailments, including such modern day problems as psoriasis.

For someone bent on getting the message out about the power of the Kingdom, Jesus' reaction raises some questions. Why did Jesus tell the man that he was not to tell anyone about what had happened to him? He was to keep the source of his new found health to himself. "See that you say nothing to anyone; but go, show yourself to the priest, and offer for your cleansing what Moses commanded, as a testimony to them."

For the record, it didn't seem to matter how strongly Jesus addressed the man. The man went right out and told everybody anyway. In fact, the word spread so fast that Jesus could no longer stay in that place. He had to go to the countryside. But that didn't take care of things either. Stories of the cures Jesus had performed reached the countryside as well, and so people from all over came looking for Jesus.

Why is Jesus so keenly intent on avoiding publicity? Or was this just a big publicity stunt in reverse? Everyone knows that the best way to spread gossip is to tell everyone a bit of juicy information, and then tell them not to say anything about it. "It's a secret." I wouldn't put that past Jesus. But I think there's something more important here than that.

It helps to remember that the leper was Jewish, as was Jesus himself. Otherwise it makes no sense to tell the man to go to the priest so that the priest can perform the necessary rituals to confirm that healing has taken place. Most likely, what's in the back of Jesus' mind is that he was afraid that the man might tell everyone *before* he went to the priest for absolution. There was, after all, a requirement in the book of Leviticus which explicitly said that it was the priest, and only the priest who could pronounce a person clean.

This was at the beginning of Jesus' ministry. Jesus was still trying to find a way to speak to his own people about what he had learned about the nature of God's Kingdom. He wanted to be on good terms with the Jewish authorities. That's why I think he told the man to keep his healing a secret. Or at least keep a secret until the man had seen the priest for testimony or proof. It was not the time or the place to shout it from the mountain tops. The healing had best be presented in the proper way to the right people at the right time. It's easy to see what Jesus is about.

The next scene in Mark 5 takes place far away from Jesus' home base. It's on the other side of the Sea of Galilee in the country known as "the Gerasenes." This was Gentile territory. Jesus had just gotten out of the boat when a man with an unclean spirit comes running up to him. The man came running from the local cemetery where he had camped out. Mark tells us that the man was out of his mind, unsafe to himself and to everyone else. The man was so wild that he could not be restrained, even with chains. No one in the village had the strength to subdue him. And besides that, the man spent his days and nights bruising himself with stones. Today, we might call him "a cutter." He obviously needed the help that Jesus could provide. When Jesus asked the man what his name was, the man replied, "Legion." A whole army of unclean spirits had taken up residence in the man's mind. Knowing what was going on inside the man's mind, Jesus commanded that the unclean spirits leave the man.

What follows is a curious story about how Jesus healed the man by driving all these unclean spirits into a herd of pigs to be drowned in the sea. Everyone came out to witness what had taken place. But what they now saw was a man completely healed inside and out. The man was sitting quietly, with his clothes on, and in his right mind. The people were so caught off guard that they didn't know quite what to make of it. So they requested that Jesus leave the area at once. They couldn't deal with such a powerful person as this. Jesus honors their request. But just as Jesus is about to get into the boat and leave, the man he has healed comes up to Jesus and begs to go with him. Jesus refuses the man's request. He tells him, "Go home to your friends, and tell them how much the Lord has done for you, and what mercy he has shown you." And the man went away and began to proclaim in the Decapolis, how much Jesus had done for him; and everyone was amazed."

Why did Jesus tell this man he healed to go and spread the good news, when he had previously told another not to? There seems to be two reasons. One reason is that this man is a Gentile and the other man is Jewish. The second reason is that now Jesus is preaching away from home, not nearby as he had previously. Jesus wants his message of God's grace to spread, but he also knows there's a time and place for everything. There's a time to speak and a time not to. Before, it was the time *not* to speak; now it's the time *to* speak.

Politicians who run for national office are sometimes accused of saying one thing in one area of the country and another thing in another part of the nation. Preachers can also be experts at this as well. I once knew a preacher who could tell liberals one thing and then use the very same words to the conservatives, but the preacher did it in a way that they both believed what the preacher had to say. They both felt the preacher was talking just to them. The reason for this is that the preacher was a master at never saying anything specific that could be pinned down. What the preacher said was so vague that both groups could read their own meaning into what was being said. It was what the groups heard and understood that made the difference, not what was actually being said. At its worst, it can be a form of what we call today, doublespeak.

Let me set the matter straight. I'm not accusing Jesus of this. Jesus preached the same message to people everywhere regardless of who they were and where he was. The content of the message was always the same. It had to do with the powerful grace of God. The message never changed. Jesus' message was not a vague, watered down, contentless message. Still, Jesus was astute enough to know that there's a time and place for everything. He told the Jewish leper he healed that it was not yet time to spread the message of God's grace publically. But to the Gentile leper, he encouraged him to go home and tell all his friends. In the Jewish areas close to his home, Jesus proceeded carefully, at least in the beginning. He even said it himself. "Everyone knows that a prophet is welcome everywhere except in his own home town." But in the Gentile areas, where the gospel did not have built-in home town opposition, Jesus could say to someone he healed to go spread the good news. Which the man did. Throughout all ten cities, in fact.

The next vignette in Mark 9 has to do with Jesus' disciples. Up until this time, Jesus has also been telling his disciples to keep quiet about what they know. Most dramatically, this is what he told the disciples at Caesarea Philippi when Peter declared that Jesus was the Messiah. "And he sternly ordered them not to tell anyone about him." But now in this episode, we learn that there will be a time when they will be able to tell everyone what they know.

The scene involves three of those closest to Jesus. These three, Peter, James and John, are the ones who make up the inner circle of Jesus' disciples. In this scene, these three are with Jesus up on the high mountain. An amazing thing took place. Jesus was transfigured. That's why today we call the place the Mount of Transfiguration. The event was a kind of beautification. We are told that Jesus' clothes were dazzling white. As Mark reports it, the clothes were so white that no bleach on earth could make them that white. And there appeared with Jesus, two greats of the Old Testament, Moses and Elijah. It is Peter who recognizes that what is happening is certainly out of the ordinary. But even though Peter knows that something magnificent is taking place, he's not quite able to make out what it means. A voice from the clouds in the heavens supplies the meaning Peter is searching for. "This is my Son, the Beloved," says the voice, "listen to him."

And once again, as he has already done before in this gospel, Jesus tells his disciples not to say anything about what they've seen and experienced. Yet this time there's a difference. There is a tip-off. The disciples learn that there will come a time when they will be able to speak openly about what has happened. After the resurrection of Jesus, they will be able to speak. For now, they are not to say anything.

Why this delay? Jesus knows that by then, they will have the confidence they need to withstand the pressures that will come to them. One day they will find all the power they need to proclaim from the rooftops who Jesus is and what his message is about. But to fill them with the courage they need, it will take nothing short of God's bringing their beloved Master back from the dead, together with a gift of the Holy Spirit.

The delay is not for naught. The disciples are being given the time they need to learn the things they will need to know once Jesus has gone. The time of silence is a time for learning. The delay is filled with purpose.

The delay can be compared to time immediately prior to an Easter Egg Hunt for children. Before everyone arrives, some of the Easter Bunny's helpers place eggs all over the grounds, some hidden very nicely, other eggs out in the open. But all eggs are placed for the same purpose: to be found. In a similar way, right now, as Jesus' disciples listen to their Master, it is the time to be hiding eggs. Come Easter morning, the Day of the Resurrection, the eggs can all be gathered up, enjoyed and shared. Everything then will be out in the open.

Have you ever played the children's game where everyone is told to keep silent? It's always interesting to see who's the first to break the silence. Surprisingly in Mark's gospel, it's not the people Jesus has healed, nor even his disciples who break the silence; it is Jesus himself. Jesus reserves the right to speak. He's the right person at the right time in the right place to say what needs to be said.

A beloved member of a congregation I once served said to me something that has stayed with me, something I have pondered many times. This is what he said: "I don't know about other congregations, but you ought to know that in this congregation, it's not been said until the Senior Minister has said it." I can't tell you how often I was reminded of that awesome responsibility. I don't even know if it's still true with regard to that congregation. For during my ministry with them, I tried to spread that responsibility out a little. But I do know that it can be true of every organization, not just the church. In any organization, there are some things that have not been said until the senior executive says it.

It's no coincidence that Jesus is the one to bring it all out into the open. During his interrogation in Mark 14, the high priest asks Jesus, "Are you the Messiah? The Son of the Blessed One?" Jesus said, "I am." Until that time, until that very moment, no one had said it out loud, or for that matter could have said it out loud. In that moment, at that time, no one but Jesus could speak the words. According to Mark, Jesus is the only one who could break the silence and proclaim the coming of God's Kingdom of Grace. So at that moment, at that time, he did.

So, what can we conclude from this brief journey through Mark's gospel? To speak or not to speak is not as easy as it might appear, or as simple as some seem to think. It all depends. It all depends on the condition, when and where. It all depends on what needs to be said or kept silent. And it depends on who is the one to say it. Or not say it. The way Mark tells the story sheds light on how we might go about it, and what kinds of things we ought to take into consideration before we open our mouths. At the very least, we might learn to think twice before we say something that we might later regret.

CHAPTER 3

WHAT MORE CAN I SAY?

Matthew 12:38-42, Mark 8:11-13, Luke 11:29-32, Luke 12:54-56, Luke 17:20-37

What Jesus said to the disciples and to the Pharisees so many years ago still haunts us. Even though these words come from a time long removed from ours, they still compel us to take notice of them. Ours is a time that is distrustful of so much, and yearns for more proof about everything. So, what are we to make of it when Jesus says to those who ask for a sign, "No sign will be given you"?

The place to begin is with what is most certainly the earliest gospel, the Gospel of Mark. In a passage from Mark 8, it is important to take notice of who is asking for a sign. Who asks a question tells you a lot even before you hear what the question is. Teachers know that. When so-and-so's hand goes up, instantly the teacher may brace herself, or take a more eager attitude to what's going to happen next. I still remember the day when the class clown asked my high school English teacher if Italy was an adverb, since it ended in -ly. Of course, now the teacher had two problems, what to do with the question, and how to restore order to the class.

So, it helps immensely to know that it's the Pharisees, Jesus' major opponents, who come up with the question about a sign from heaven. Why they felt they needed any more proof than they already had is puzzling. After all, this was after the feeding of the 4000, along with several healings by Jesus. Perhaps the Pharisees were not present at these times. But if they had not been there when Jesus worked these miracles, they surely had heard about them from others who were. These things were "not done in a corner," as the scriptures put it.

No, this demand for a sign was simply to discredit Jesus. The Pharisees were trying to test him. They had already made up their minds about Jesus, and now they were looking for another opportunity to make him look foolish in the sight of the crowd. So they say, "Teacher, we wish to see a sign from you." And Jesus, just as adamantly, replies, "… no sign will be given." Significantly, after this, Jesus withdraws from their presence, and effectively ends his missionary activity in Galilee.

This is the story of how it all took place according to Mark. In Mark, the refusal of Jesus is absolute, final: There will be no sign. The religious leaders of his day do not deserve one. They have shown that by their attitudes and actions. And besides, they have had plenty of signs already.

In the seventh chapter of Mark, verse 34, Jesus lets out a groan as he's healing a deaf and dumb man. Then in the verse from Chapter 8, Jesus sighs deeply over the way the Pharisees are not accepting his message from God. It's as if Jesus is saying to them, "What more can I say?" In Mark's gospel, from this point on, Jesus will turn away from the public and devote his time and energy completely to his small band of followers.

When we come to Matthew's gospel, things are pretty much the same, but with a twist. Now, when asked for a sign by the Pharisees, Jesus replies, "… no sign will be given to it except the sign of prophet Jonah." Both the gospel of Mark and the gospel of Matthew acknowledge Jesus' refusal to answer the request for a sign with more miracles. But in Matthew, we now have this interesting qualification: There will be no sign, except the sign of Jonah. What's this all about?

For Matthew, Jonah's experience in the belly of a big fish for three days and nights is symbolic of Jesus' three days in the tomb before the resurrection. For Matthew, everything will become clear after the resurrection. The disciples will not know until later what it all means. The point of the gospel message, however, remains the same. There is a need for repentance, for a changing of their minds and hearts. Jonah was given a message by God to preach to Nineveh. The message was that things must change. The people couldn't continue to go on the way they were. Repent and believe in God was the message. And, just about as miraculously as staying alive in the belly of a great fish for three days, the people of Nineveh listened to what Jonah had to say. They repented and turned around their lives.

The message becomes even more intense when we come to the account in Luke's gospel. The sign of Jonah appears to refer to Jesus himself. At least, that's what Luke seems to be pointing to later in Chapter 17:20-21. There Jesus says, "You cannot tell by observation when the kingdom of God comes. There will be no saying, 'Look, here it is! Or "there it is!"; for in fact the kingdom of God is among you.'" (NEB)

It's not always possible to tell what a sign means. In the movie, *Signs*, there is a scene where the whole town is trying to make sense out of what is happening to them. Mysterious patterns are showing up in the cornfields. Who or what made them? Some see it one way, others another. The people's reactions to Jesus' ministry were pretty much the same as in the movie.

And at this juncture in his mission, Jesus is rejecting the need for more miraculous proof. At this stage in the game, it would take away from his power and presence, not add to it. Jesus wants people to deal with *him*, not what he's saying and doing.

In Luke, the message is still basically the same. No sign will be given, certainly not the kind you might expect, let alone want. And this time, Jesus is harder on the Pharisees than before. In Chapter 12:54-56, it is as if Jesus tells them, "You seem to be very good at interpreting the weather. How come you cannot read the signs of the times that are right before you? You are the designated religious leaders. Why can't you see what's going on?"

Are we not like the Pharisees? Don't we each want our own little private assurances instead of being content with the basic message that's for everyone? Have you noticed how some people can never seem to get what the preacher is saying until they've personally had a chance to ask what it means? Sometimes the question is a genuine thirst to know more. But sometimes it appears to be more like grabbing for a piece of clothing from a rock star celebrity.

Those around at the time were doing the same with Jesus. And when he tells them that no sign will be given, it's as if he's saying, "What do you want from me? What more can I say than I've already said? I've said it all before. Do you still not get it?" But they simply refuse to pay attention. They will not listen to what he's telling them. That's why no sign will be given.

But more can still be said. At least Luke seems to think so, particularly in Chapter 17. Chapter 17 is a companion story. We hear about Noah and the flood, Lot and Sodom. We also learn about that day when there will be no time to pick up one's belongings, much as if there's a fire in your hotel and you have to evacuate the room immediately. Some will be taken from the bed while others are not. There is talk about vultures gathering around the corpse. What does this have to do with anything?

As I've lived with these scriptures for the last few years, this is the way I've come to see it. I think Jesus is saying something like this. "If you really think that you have to have a sign, then you'll simply have to wait. When the times comes, you'll know. When it happens, you will know. But not a moment before." Many times we only know what it all means when we look back on it.

Back in the 70's, our denomination, The Christian Church (Disciples of Christ), chose for its Regional Minister in Indiana, Dr. John Compton. Dr. Compton was the first African-American to hold that office. During his term of service, a decision was made that pictures of ministerial candidates would no longer be attached to the relocation forms. Today this is standard practice almost everywhere in our church and others. I recall what Dr. Compton had to say when he was asked by a search committee how they were going to know if a candidate were black or white, now that there were no pictures to go by. In his characteristic way of good humor, Dr. Compton replied, "Believe me, when they show up, you'll know!" And Jesus would add, not a moment before.

The hard truth is, there are times in our lives when we simply have to wait to find out what it's all about: whether we've gotten the job, passed the test, made the grade, or won the election. These are only some of the times. There are many, many more. At these times, no sign will be given until the results are in.

While we were in England on sabbatical in 2004, my wife, Susan, and I were enthralled with how the English were voting by mail ballot. We thought that surely they must have learned something from us Americans in the prior presidential election in Florida. Evidently not. Looking back, I guess it turned out all right for them. With regard to those elected to the European Union, the British elections were held several days before the rest of the countries in the Union. The results of the British elections had to be kept secret until all the rest were announced. In this way the British elections would not unduly affect the outcome in other countries. In the meantime, the British people simply had to wait to find out. Yes, there was some premature guessing by the press, but not nearly as much as might be expected. And certainly not as much as in the U.S. with exit polls and media coverage before election votes are tallied. What struck us, though, was how patient the British people seemed to be to wait to find out what was what.

On the other hand, Susan and I watched in dismay the big game on TV as the English football team lost to the French in the last, 137th minute. They had been ahead for most of the game. "The English deserved to win," was the way David Beckham, their star captain, put it to the TV interviewer. But then, in the end, the French had outwitted them. As with all contests, there is no way to know who wins until the game is over. As Yogi Berra says, "It's not over 'till it's over." It's not over until the results are in, and "the fat lady sings." And that's that.

But we human beings are never content with this. We're always trying to force God's hand. We want to make the future arrive before its time. To this Jesus says, "No sign will be given." Except this: You will know it when you see it. And besides, what more can I say?

CHAPTER 4

SETTING A PRECEDENT

**Matthew 26:6-13, Mark 10:21, Mark 14:3-9,
Luke 7:36-50, John 12:1-8**

The story of the Anointing of Jesus is one of the few stories that can be found in all four gospels. That in itself, points to its widespread significance.

However, when compared with other teachings and stories of Jesus, this story immediately becomes puzzling. For instance, place this story about the lavish expense of perfume side-by-side with the one commonly referred to as the Rich Young Ruler. In the Rich Young Ruler, Jesus says in no uncertain terms, "Go, sell what you have and give it to the poor." How do we square these apparently contradictory words with the extravagant actions displayed by the woman who spills the costly perfume? On the surface, aren't the objections raised about the misuse of this costly ointment more in line with what Jesus has said on the earlier occasions? Or is the story simply one of a kind, and speaks only about this woman individually? If so, could we not say the same with regard to the Rich Young Ruler? Specifically, why does Jesus not only consent to what the woman is doing, but applauds it? Are there times when it's OK to be lavish and extravagant? And if so, what are these times? And when should we give to the poor? How do we know which way to go? Always and at all times? Or, as this woman's actions suggest, are there times when we are called to attend to more important matters? In a word, are there circumstances that justify, even call for, such a radical departure from the expected normal practices of charity?

Furthermore, given our own feelings about all this, how do we, ourselves, "sort these things out," as the Brits like to say? In order to answer that question, recall how those present at the time felt about it. After all, this incident was not above being questioned when it first happened. It's instructive that the gospel writers, each in their own way, decided to sign in on what they felt that the audience might be feeling as it read or heard this story.

In Luke's gospel, Simon is the host. But interestingly, Simon is silent on the matter. You might think that the host would feel some responsibility for what had happened in his home. He might just feel called upon to be the spokesperson for everyone present. But instead, Simon is as quiet as a mouse. Could it be that Simon is a converted follower of Jesus and understands his master's deeds more than it might seem? In other places in the gospels, we hear about Simon the Leper whom Jesus had cured. Is this the same Simon? And if so, is Simon's reticence due to the fact that he is so grateful for what Jesus has done for him that he can appreciate Jesus' understanding of what the woman has done? How can Simon ever repay Jesus for his new found health, health which not only allows him to mingle freely with the townspeople, attend Temple services, but also invite people into his house for a dinner party? Looked at in this way, it's not too much of a stretch to see why Simon is not speaking out against Jesus while the others are.

In Matthew's version of the incident, the disciples corporately are upset with the woman's actions in spilling the costly perfume. Together, they feel that this lavish act is uncalled for and the perfume could better have been used in a wiser way to aid those less fortunate.

In Mark's take on the story, the blow is softened. Mark reports the goings on indirectly, as is his habit. We learn that "some" objected, no doubt including the disciples. But Mark is gracious enough not to point it out. Maybe even he, himself, was one of those who protested.

In John's account, the details vary even more. This variety has led some to conclude that John is speaking of an all-together different occasion involving another woman. John singles out Judas as the one who singly raised the question. The same story or not, it's quite likely that Judas was the one to have been the most offended. Being the treasurer of the funds of this little band of disciples, Judas would have borne the responsibility for handling the money for the group. Is this not something that we have come to expect from our treasurers? How many times have we not heard a treasurer raise the question: "Isn't there something better we could be doing with this money?" Yes, it is convincing that it was Judas who voiced the concern. However, later generations of Christians probably went too far in thinking that his motives were perverse. Judas did not have to be the devil's tool or even act solely out of greed to raise the question. Good, faithful Christians can come up with that one on their own, and still do.

At any rate, this must have been an exceptional case to warrant such an event even taking place. I recall one Christmas when members of our family decided that we would only give presents to the children and not to the adults. The reason behind the decision made perfect sense. We adults certainly didn't need anything. So why waste good money on something we didn't need? But come Christmas morning, when there were no gifts for us grownups to open, both the giver and the receiver were cheated out of a blessing. To top it off, by our decision, we adults taught another lesson that we were not intending, and that was that Christmas is only for children. How do you explain that to a young child who wants to know why the rest of us are not receiving any gifts? What can you say that will get them to understand? You can't. Nor did it work for one of my friends who announced that he didn't want any presents for Christmas. Instead, he wanted his family to donate to their favorite charity the amount that they would have spent on him. They all agreed, but my friend said that come Christmas morning, when all gathered around the tree, everyone could sense that there was something wrong. He said he could not quite put his finger on what went wrong. It's that "something wrong" that needs to be pinned down. Something else must be going on in this moving story to be included in all four gospels.

So what about our own objections? That's the question that earlier was held at bay until we took a look at the objections recorded in the story itself. Isn't what the woman in the story did almost unforgivable? Spilling all that costly perfume, when it could have done so much more good in the world, isn't that a sheer waste?

I, for one, hate to see most anything wasted. I shudder when I think of how much food I leave on my plate when I go to a restaurant these days. I almost always come home with a doggy bag to avoid the waste and assuage my guilt. But either way, whether I eat it there or take it home and eat it later, it's still food that I didn't need and would have been so much better given to someone who did need it.

I also don't like to see something beautiful trashed, like breaking an expensive, alabaster vase that was no doubt a delight to behold. I can hardly bear to see someone put their feet on a polished wood coffee table. Years ago, when I was counseling a group of young scouts for their God and Country Award, they met after school in the living room of the parsonage. To a boy they persisted in putting their feet on our parquet coffee table. One day when I had had it, I said, "Now, you would never do that at home, would you? Why do you do it here?" I could see by the looks on their faces that they didn't have the least idea of what I was talking about.

I confess I love beautiful things. I love to go to art museums and castles and cathedrals to see all the lavish works of inspired artists through the centuries. Even an old Southern boy like me appreciates the use of a silver tea set at wedding receptions and anniversaries. Forgive me, animal rights activists, but there is still something in me that admires a woman in a full-length mink coat, as many ladies in the church wore at the time I grew up, not to speak of glamorous film stars. Something in me understands what was in that woman's heart that made her do what she did for Jesus.

So however little or big, even if it's difficult to get rid of our objections, even after we've tried to understand each of the characters in the story, it's still not easy to understand what the story is saying and asking us to do.

But enough of speculations and objections and secret longings and yearnings. What light can the scriptures themselves shed on our dilemma?

First of all, we can rule out one way of getting off the hook. Calvin's way was to suggest that what Jesus said to the rich young ruler only applied to him and to him alone. But this is not acceptable. There is nothing in the text to suggest this restriction. This is just another example of a great theologian reading his own personal desires into an otherwise plain text. It reminds me of what a young minister said to her treasurer after he made a comment to her upon her arrival to the church. The treasurer remarked that the congregation she had come to serve was not wealthy and did not like to hear much about money. Without any reflection whatsoever, the new minister found herself saying, "Well, isn't that convenient!" Rather than being offended by what she said, the treasurer let out a big roar of laughter. "Got ya!" Sometimes we like to be got. Especially at those times when we know that we should be. Someone should have had the nerve to have told old Calvin that. Standing before Jesus, we are all rich young men. And that means we are also all potentially devoted women bearing lavish gifts. Neither of these stories is an isolated case. They are for us to deal with and to learn from.

It's helpful to realize that there were actually two kinds of gifts that were deemed acceptable in first century Israel. There were gifts of justice and gifts of mercy. Gifts of justice were almsgiving, and they had to do with looking after the poor. Gifts of mercy, on the other hand, covered things like how to appropriately care for the dead. In essence, the gift the woman in the story made surpassed a gift of almsgiving. Her gift was a gift of mercy dedicated to the one, unknown at the moment even to her, as One who would shortly die.

There is also a distinction to be made between personal commitment to a known person and the general duty to take care of the anonymously needy. Jesus is right when he says that the poor will always be with us. That's the reason we should always be looking after them. But there are times when there's something else we need to do. There's a matter of a hierarchy of importance of gifts. I'm hesitant to use the word, but I can think of no better way to speak of this than to use the word "ladder" to describe what's going on. Echoing the pioneering New Testament scholar, Jeremias, W.T. Davies concludes, "the disciples preferred giving of alms to waste; Jesus preferred love to alms."[1] The rungs on the ladder move up from waste to alms to love. So what may appear to be waste is actually love. Love is extravagant. This is one thing we like about love. It's abundant and lavish.

And then there is the significance of the one for whom the deed is being done. That's what went wrong when our family did not get Christmas presents for the adults and my friend suggested his family give to charity instead. The one for whom the gift is intended somehow gets lost along the way. Even with the best intentions, there's something not quite right about it. And everyone can feel it.

Jesus applauds the woman for "the fine thing" she has done. Breaking the expensive alabaster vase containing priceless perfume from far off India and anointing Jesus' body with the oil, turns out to be just as "fine a thing" as giving to the poor. In fact, the same Greek word that is used for "a fine thing" is the very word scripture uses to describe acts of mercy. Words of scripture invite us to understand the meaning from the inside out. However that day, the disciples and all present, everyone except Jesus and the woman, were looking at the act from the outside in.

What then do these two seemingly antithetical scriptures have in common? What is it that transcends them and points to a greater paradoxical truth? Both the rich young ruler and the woman with the jar of ointment indicate two responses of commitment to Jesus. In the first, Jesus calls for a total response. The rich young man is to step up to a deeper level of commitment. Why? Because Jesus loves him and wants him to experience the inner joys of eternal life. On the other hand, the woman loves Jesus so much that Jesus does not have to command, much less even ask, for her commitment

---

1   W.D. Davies and Dale C. Allison Jr., *Matthew Vol 3*, Edinburgh: T&T Clark 1991, p446

and devotion. She spills it out for all to see, letting its fragrance fill the air.

And there is still another hint at what's being laid out for us to see. Rather than living our lives by the check book, calculating how much we'll spend for this and what amount of money we will give to that, we see instead what love is capable of when unleashed from mechanical deliberations. Why, from the moment she entered the room, this woman had actually been flaunting her conversion, daring to enter the place where men were eating even before they were finished with their meal. She even added to the confusion, by squandering what amounts to a year's income in one questionable gesture! Why? To anoint Jesus in advance for his burial, as we will learn.

So what are our options when it comes to living the Christian life? Are we to write a check for the poor who will always be with us? Or in those special moments when we have a window of opportunity, by our actions tell Jesus and all we love how much we love them? Yes. There doesn't always have to be a choice, as the disciples, and especially Judas, seem to think. Only be awake to the opportunity when it presents itself.

The woman with the costly vase of nard intuitively knew that this was her one and only chance to let Jesus know how much she loved him. Her act was unsolicited, impulsive, but not entirely unplanned. After all, she had to arrange to bring the vase with her to Simon's house. What counts was that she was able to discern the meaning of what was going on right before her, something that the others were unable to do. Or better put, she knew that Jesus would understand even if the others did not. She knew that Jesus would get the point, and that's all that mattered.

Does love always have to stop to think things out? Interestingly, Mark is the only gospel that mentions the breaking of the jar. Arguably, that act in itself was one of total, unabashed commitment. It's a one time event, never to be repeated again. In this story, I never get the feeling that this is the kind of woman who goes around doing these kinds of crazy things. If she did, I doubt that the story would have made it into one gospel, much less four.

That's why her story is remembered to this day, just as Jesus said it would be. Unknowingly, she had anointed Jesus' body in advance of his burial. Maybe that's the reason Jesus sides with her against his own disciples. They would have known that it was customary to pour a little oil on the hair of guests in the house of a wealthy dinner party that day. But what she did was absolutely unprecedented! She bathed Jesus in perfume. And on that day, by her unprecedented act, she set the precedent for Christians for all time, leaving us with an example of what it means to "love him who first loved us."

CHAPTER 5
POWER PLAYS

Mark 10:35-45

I t's sure to happen. You can count on it. A beloved minister leaves the church whether through choice or pressure or retirement. A problem arises. There is now a potential vacuum of leadership. Who will lead the congregation? That's the overwhelming question. You can bet that not too long after the announcement of the change in leadership is made, certain individuals will begin jockeying for power. A power play, overt or covert, subtle or out in the light of day for all to see, begins to take shape. Sometimes it's as abrupt as a coup. At other times, it is more subdued, behind the scene. Sometimes it's political. There are those who make sure that they (or someone they know) will be on the search committee charged to come up with the next potential leader, hopefully a leader that they can approve and possibly influence.

And this kind of dynamic is not confined to the church. It happens in most any kind of organization: governmental, educational, health care or political. It often becomes apparent during the so-called 'lame duck' period of the U.S. Presidency. For the time being, possible candidates refrain from lashing out at the opposition outside their party and begin taking pot shots at former colleagues within their own party. At its worst, there is name-calling, backbiting, and distancing from other candidates, whom they may have claimed as good friends only weeks or months before. Simply put, the game is this: "I want to make sure that I'm the next candidate for my party, and not you."

Or on a more personal, intimate scale this grasping for power can infect families. An older child moves out of the house to go off to college or perhaps get married. If there are other children in the family, the question of who gets the now vacated room becomes uppermost in the minds of those left behind. It doesn't even have to be the children. There's a TV commercial where the father and mother are pining about how they're going to miss their daughter who has just left for college, all the while imagining how they will use her room for themselves. Father says, "I'll get the paint. You get the wallpaper." Mother says, "I have dibs on the desk." Father replies, "I have dibs on the teddy bear." The scenario is innocently played out, I suspect, until the daughter comes home to find that she no longer has a place to lay her head. There is literally now no room for her at home.

Sometimes, if the loss is due to a death of the family member, the reaction can be more severe and pronounced. Many times it's overladen with guilt. The room of the beloved becomes a shrine and nothing is to be removed. The power play now is to show that one family member loves the deceased more than the rest. "Mom, if you really loved Dad, you wouldn't even think of dating so soon."

I guess you could say that this kind of experience has been with us from the beginning of time. No sooner had Moses gone up to Mount Sinai than the people of Israel demanded that Aaron, second in command, take over and make a golden calf for them to fall down before and worship. And according to the winsome BBC series, *Robin Hood*, the whole ploy of stealing from the rich and giving to the poor began when Robin returned home from serving King Richard in the Crusades, and found that a wicked sheriff had usurped his position in Nottingham. Yes, these kinds of power plays are nothing new. But just because they have been around for a long time, does not mean that they should just be left alone to play themselves out.

How to respond to experiences of vacancy and loss in life becomes the issue. And sometimes, it's hard to know how to respond, because the dynamics of the interlude become so muddled and confused. What's called for is a detached view of the matter, a more objective perspective on what's going on. Yet that's the one thing involved members of the family, church, or political party cannot do for themselves.

A more detached perspective is needed. Say, like the one Jesus had with his disciples that day when they were on the road to Jerusalem. Jesus could see what his disciples could not see. Specifically, Jesus could see what James and John could not. And this is the first lesson to be pointed out. It takes an outside observer to see what's going on in the interaction that makes up a power play. Those involved are too close to the action to know what's really transpiring. Those involved in a power play often think that they have the whole picture, when in truth, they only see part of it. That explains why those who are successful in placing themselves in positions of leadership during an interim, often find that their ideas for change fail to pan out in the way they had hoped. The disenchanted most usually seize upon the part of the job that is most congenial to them, not the part that may actually be needed.

In Mark's version of the incident, James and John, sons of Zebedee, come up to Jesus, who has been walking ahead of them as was the custom of a rabbi and his students while traveling. They say to Jesus, "Teacher, we want you to do for us whatever we ask of you." Isn't that about the most blatant request you've ever heard? In front of God and everybody, these two have the gall to ask Jesus to do something that they haven't even told him what they want him to do. These two are like little children trying to get their parents to promise something before they tell the parents what it is. James and John bring the question up in a round-about-way. "Do for us what we ask of you." As if to say, "Give us the credit card to use before we tell you what we want to buy with it." Jesus could have said, "You've got to be kidding? Are you out of your mind? No way!" But Jesus knows these two disciples better than they know themselves. He knows them from the inside out, having spent the better part of three years with them. So he goes along with them. "What is it that you want me to do for you?" And now we hear it from their very own lips. "Grant us to sit, one at your right hand and one at your left, in your glory." But Jesus said to them, "You do not know what you are asking."

Once, when I was serving as president of a healthcare facility, some members of the board came to me with some concerns, more like complaints, about the current CEO. After listening to their gripes, I consulted a very wise man on the board who had been around the block a few times. I told him of their concerns, not mentioning the names of those who had raised the questions. His response was quick and to the point. "Put anybody in the chair of the CEO and these people will have the same concerns and complaints about that person. It comes with the position. They do not know what they're asking."

Actually, what we are talking about, and what Jesus recognized in the request of James and John, is that we all have a blind spot. A blind spot is literally a *blind* spot. We don't know it's there because we cannot see it. There is a good reason why the spot on the driver's side of the car is called a blind spot. Another car can be right beside the driver and the driver can be completely unaware of it. Neither the side mirror nor the rearview mirror will be able to detect it. Unless the driver changes perspective by turning around and looking over his shoulder, the approaching car cannot be seen. If this is not done, especially before moving into another lane of traffic, there is a potential for a collision. Jesus knew that James and John had a blind spot when it came to his ministry and mission. That's why he said to them, "You do not know what you are asking."

It is helpful to put this passage from Mark in its immediate context. This passage follows the magnificent event called The Transfiguration. James and John were with Jesus that day, as was Peter, when Jesus' presence was transformed before their eyes. They heard God give Jesus both approval and authority for the mission he was to carry out. Also, it was not too long after that, that James and John, along with the other disciples, found that they were not able to exorcise demons as their Master had commissioned them. This was demoralizing, to say the least. But now, as they are on the road to Jerusalem, there is the thrill of approaching the Holy City. They are all pumped up for what they think might transpire. Jesus is finally coming into his own. He would shortly be recognized as the leader they knew he was. Yes, there had been some repeated mention of Jesus going to die in Jerusalem. They had heard Jesus mention it at least three times recently. But these two disciples, especially, didn't take it seriously. James and John were blind to this as a real possibility. So they seized upon what was pleasing to them personally. Jesus was going to be King, and they wanted to be his chief assistants.

"Could we have the best jobs?"

"You don't know what you are asking. Are you able to drink the cup that I drink, or to be baptized with the baptism that I am baptized with?"

They replied, "We are able."

How blind can one be? How imperceptive? Yet once more Jesus does not say, "You fools!" as he well might have. Instead he replies, "The cup that I drink you will drink; and the baptism with which I am baptized, you will be baptized; ..." Jesus tells them that it won't be too long before they themselves will be in trouble because of their association with him. The truth is, to sit at Jesus' right or left is not up to him, but to God. Ironically, as some have pointed out, when Jesus is crucified, it's not these two disciples who are on his right and left, but two criminals who were also crucified that day. At the crucifixion, the disciples, including both James and John, were nowhere to be found.

Mark also gives us a picture of the reaction of the other disciples who overheard James and John's request. It seems that the other disciples became quite angry when they heard this. It's not exactly clear why they were angry. But could it be, as some have suggested, that they had been upstaged? Had James and John got the jump on them? Did they get to Jesus first with their request?

Jesus, ever the hands-on teacher, takes the occasion to give some on-the-spot lessons in the meaning of true leadership. It's what is known today as servant leadership. "You know that among the Gentiles those whom they recognize as their rulers lord it over them, and their great ones are tyrants over them. But it is not so among you; but whoever wishes to become great among you must be your servant, and whoever wishes to be first among you must be a slave of all." Applying the principle to himself, Jesus goes on to say, "For the Son of Man came not to be served but to serve, and to give his life in ransom for many."

What had happened and how it came about had to be addressed. Jesus knew that this lesson could not be put off until later. Time was running out. Not fixing things now, meant that they would never be fixed. The system needed changing. Certainly, there was no time for quarrels about status. There were more important matters at hand, matters of life and death.

If it's possible to ferret out what Jesus is trying to tell his disciples, and thus saying to us more modern day types, it's that old ways of thinking about leadership no longer apply. James and John were still thinking about ancient hierarchical ladders and positions of power. Jesus is taking a more egalitarian way of looking at things.

In John's gospel, there is the ultimate example. It comes when Jesus puts a towel around his waist and washes the disciples' feet. And that night, it was not James and John who didn't get it, but Peter, who had always been the recognized team leader of the group.

A side bar: Isn't it interesting that in their quest for power, James and John are willing to push aside the most likely candidate for their next leader—Peter? And isn't it even more interesting that as far as we know, Peter never takes them on for their action. In that astute way, Peter demonstrates, at that moment, a deeper understanding of true leadership than these two.

A wholesale reorientation about life in general and leadership in particular is laid out for us. It is set before us clearly and persuasively in this story about two ambitious brothers. Overarching all that's going on, in, with, and under, is the recognition that the values of Jesus and his mission are not the same as those of the world. There is a Grand Reversal. The values of the world are turned upside down. This story of the request of James and John is one of the clearest examples of this reorientation to be found anywhere in the gospels.

Astounding, perhaps, and even more reassuring, is that Jesus accepts these two blind disciples as still having a part to play in his mission. But with that said, Jesus has a more wide-eyed, yet realistic view. In a nut shell, the mission here on earth is to serve others. Greatness is to be found in service, not in positions of honor and glory. Greatness is to follow the lead of the leader who condescends to wash the feet of those who are trying to be just like him.

One beautiful Fall morning, I was attending a convention of our denomination. That morning, several hundred of us who were attending descended upon the breakfast room of the hotel where we were staying. We all arrived at the last minute. We pushed the capacity of the room way beyond the fire marshal's stated limit. In the process, we drove the nerves of the servers beyond distraction by our many requests, requests which all came down to "Me, first!" While the rest of us were trying to make sure that we were being served first so that we could get the best seats on the convention floor, the president of one of our prominent seminaries, virtually known by all not only for the position he held, but also for his impeccable grooming, went over to a server, and whispered into her ear. After she nodded a 'yes' in reply, this grand, Christian statesman picked up a pot of coffee and proceeded to serve all of us gripers and complainers until our orders could be taken. Someone cynical could say that it was all for show. But I, for one, have not seen a better, more practical, example of servant leadership, before or since. And it has been a very long time, indeed, since that early morning breakfast. Yet the memory lasts.

Jesus said, "You know how it is with others. But it is not so with you." And in saying that, he *ruled out* all kinds of power plays in all kinds of places for all time. And do I even need to say it again positively? Probably not, but I can't resist. By saying what he did, Jesus *ruled in* a life of service for all, by all, forever, on earth, as it is in heaven. Amen.

CHAPTER 6

A PUBLIC OR PRIVATE AFFAIR?

Matthew 6:1-18, Matthew 18:20

Where do we meet God? Are there some privileged places where we are more likely to make contact? Specifically, are we more likely to meet God when we are all alone by ourselves or when we are gathered together with others? Is the experience of the divine a private or a public affair? A case can and has been made for both ways. But what ultimately concerns us is what Jesus has to say about it.

A modern philosopher has said that religion is what we do with our solitude. In this view, spirituality takes place when we are all alone by ourselves. Taken at face value, this view seems to have little appreciation for the social function that religion plays in the lives of individuals, not to speak of the role it serves in the community at large. Yet, at first glance, Jesus might appear to be on this side. "But whenever you pray, go into your room and shut the door and pray to your Father who is in secret; and your Father who sees in secret will reward you." But in the very same gospel, later on we hear a promise of Jesus that suggests otherwise. "For where two or three are gathered in my name, I am there among them."

Which is it? Where are we most likely to meet God? Is a religious experience primarily public or private? Does it take place when we are off by ourselves in quiet contemplation or when we are gathered with others who are seeking him as diligently as we are? If I had to answer that question right now, I would say that it is most likely both. My own personal experience confirms the wisdom of both locations as privileged places to be in God's presence.

There have been times when I sensed God's presence in the quiet stillness of silent, solitary prayer said by a lakeside on a beautiful early summer morning. But there have also been times when I have been graced by a sense of the presence of the Holy in the joyous celebration of corporate worship, particularly on Easter Day when an overflowing church is singing powerful hymns accompanied by organ and brass. What is the difference, if there is one? And why the seeming difference, if not in simply appreciating the many differing ways it's possible to come into the presence of the Almighty?

It could be that when these two passages from Matthew, and the verses surrounding them, are examined a bit more closely, it is possible to see that these scriptures speak of two complimentary avenues to encountering the same one, true and holy God.

For starters, the passage about going into a room and shutting the door and locking it is not so much a matter of shutting the world out as to protect ourselves from the temptation to make a show of our faith. Isn't this the main point of Matthew 6:1-18? In these verses, Jesus is not actually against public displays of faith, only their misuse. Jesus knows that when we remove ourselves from the scene it does not guarantee that we will use our faith wisely, but it does go a long way to insure the possibility.

When we are in solitude with God, we are not as vulnerable to the "look at me" temptation. That is, unless we take pains to make sure that everyone knows what we're doing when we are off by ourselves. A well-known spiritual guide once advised ministers as to what their secretaries should tell those who were bent on seeking the pastor's attention. "The pastor is not available right now; the pastor is with God." What does that kind of advice convey to the parishioner's feelings of being pushed away? There is a danger of sending the wrong message. "Look at me, I'm the pastor! And I'm praying with God right now. I'm much too busy to be with you." Human beings seem to have a basic instinct to fall into these kinds of traps. It's one of those feelings that goes back to childhood. "Daddy, look at me. See how fast I can go down the big slide! Did you see me, Mommy?" For the record, Jesus is against all forms of ostentation and parading of our religion around for people to see.

"Beware of practicing your piety before others in order to be seen by them; for then you have no reward from your Father in heaven."

But Jesus does not just stop with a warning; he goes on to show us how to do it. Jesus outlines various ways of handling the matter. Actually, there are three basic ways to live out our faith, back then and right now. These three are giving of alms, prayer and fasting. Basically, Jesus says that we are not to toot our own horn with regard to all of these. I don't know who first put it this way, but it has stuck with me. "Blessed are those who toot-eth not their own horns, for theirs shall be tooted!" Maybe for some people it's as simple as not hanging out on the church steps to make sure that everyone who drives by will see them. Indeed, "... when you give alms, do not let your left hand know what your right hand is doing, so that your alms may be done in secret; and your Father who sees in secret will reward you.... But whenever you fast, do not look dismal, like the hypocrites, for they disfigure their faces so as to show others that they are fasting. Truly, I tell you they have received their reward." In all of these instances, Jesus astutely observes that no heavenly rewards await, for the earthly awards have been claimed already.

The longer we reflect upon these passages, the more apparent it is that Jesus values inward serenity over outward display. Jesus prefers matters of the heart over external appearances. And most of all, he applauds earnest desire for God's approval over the approval of other human beings like ourselves.

So much is this the case, that the pages of the New Testament are filled with pictures of Jesus all alone with God in prayer. In the earliest gospel, Mark, in the very first chapter we read that "while it was still very dark, he (Jesus) got up and went out to a deserted place, and there he prayed" (Mark 1:35). Again in the same gospel immediately after the famous walking-on-water episode, Jesus "after saying farewell to them, went up on the mountain to pray" (Mark 6:46). And on that tragic night when he was betrayed to the authorities, we see Jesus going to a place called Gethsemane. And he said to his disciples, "Sit here while I pray" (Mark 14:32).

Luke touches on the same devotional practices. After healing a leper, again in his customary way, Jesus withdraws "to deserted place to pray" (Luke 5:16). In fact, Luke tells us that the day before Jesus chose the twelve to be his disciples, Jesus had "spent the night in prayer to God" (Luke 6:12). And on two other rather dramatic occasions, Jesus is all alone in prayer: once before Peter's historic confession of Jesus as the Messiah of God, and then again during the miraculous transfiguration. "And while he was praying, the appearance of his face changed, and his clothes became dazzling white" (Luke 9:29).

However, when attention is concentrated solely on Jesus's personal prayer life, it is possible to lose sight of his support of public religion. It should not be forgotten that Jesus taught in synagogues, attended wedding feasts, and observed religious celebrations, such as Passover (e.g., Mark 6:2, John 2, Luke 22). In one story of the healing of a woman who had been suffering from a hemorrhage for twelve years, it is mentioned in passing that she came up from behind Jesus and touched the fringe of his cloak. While not all interpreters agree, some see significance in the presence of this fringe on Jesus' robe. It suggests that even Jesus was not above having some outward display of religious beliefs on his person. Whether or not Jesus was actually a Pharisee is still being debated, however.

In light of all this information, just how serious are we to take this going into a private room and locking the door behind us? Is the gesture symbolic or literal? Or both? One indication that it can be taken somewhat literally is the choice of the designated room itself. At the time, most residences would have had at most one room that could be locked. This was a windowless storeroom where any valuables the family might own could be kept. And symbolically, perhaps Jesus is saying that it is no little thing that we are doing when we go off by ourselves. We are retiring to the most valuable spot in the house to be with the Most Valuable Person in our lives.

Whatever else we say about prayer, its main purpose is for God. We do not pray to others, only in their presence at times. Prayer is not intended for a human audience. So anything that gets in the way of our meeting God is to be managed in a way that helps us get in touch with God. It has often been said, prayer is not to inform God of our desires and wises, but to cleanse our minds and hearts, and align our wills with God's will.

So again, which is it? Is religion, and prayer specifically, what we do with our solitude? Is it simply a private affair? Or is there a public aspect as well? In a word, what about those times when two or three are gathered together in his name?

The image of two or three goes back to the practices and teachings of rabbis. The classic instance is this: "But if two or three sit together and the words of the Law are spoken between them, the Divine presence rests between them."[1]

Is God only present when one human being is alone? Obviously not. Yes, Jesus urges us to go alone by ourselves. For there is much value in that and a great deal of reason for it. And as if we needed more than his word for it, the gospels give us an abundance of examples of how Jesus practiced what he preached. But we also see some very public displays of religious behavior on his behalf. What's at stake here?

It all has to do with integrity. Jesus wants us to make sure that whatever we do, our outward actions match our inward sensibilities. Whether we are all alone by ourselves or gathered together with God's people, we are to be ourselves. Whatever we do in public or private, we are not to be found playacting.

I can tell you how it came about for me recently. I was attending a community worship service. Because of prior experience with these kinds of gatherings, I knew, for certain, that there would be an offering. And it would be for a good cause. I decided in advance the amount I was going to give. But as I was sitting alone in my pew, some close acquaintances spotted me and asked if they could join me. Much to my delight, I welcomed them to sit with me for the service. Then it came time for the offering to be collected. As I reached for my wallet and was about to take out my offering, a thought ran through my mind. "What are these good friends of mine going to think of what I'm giving? Will it be too small or too

1   W.D. Davies and Dale C. Allison Jr., *Matthew Vol. 2*, Edinburgh: T&T Clark 1991, p 789.

large in their eyes?" Trying to put the thought out of my mind, just as the plate was about to be passed to me, I decided then and there that I would give as I had already decided before the service, before my friends came into the picture. And, if by chance, they saw what I gave and had a problem with it, that was their problem, not mine. In truth, I had already decided before God in the locked door of my heart what I was going to do. That is what mattered in this moment of public celebration, not someone else's outward impression of me.

Tom Wright, Bishop of Durham, has a way of speaking beautifully about these concerns. In his commentary on Matthew, are these penetrating words: "The point is to do business with God, one on one... What is clear is that he (Jesus) is inviting his followers to a life in which inside and outside match perfectly, because both are focused on God who sees in secret."[1]

The age we live in is a great one to ferret out hypocrites. The media is constantly on the attack to find out if everyone is who they say they are. Sadly, when they are, it's rarely pointed out. But if there is even the slightest hint of a discrepancy, you can bet that this information will find its way into the evening news. These days I cannot but wonder if the spotlight is being focused on each and every one of us Christians.

Finally it's not whether it's a private or a public affair so much as if we are the same in public as we are in private. It is a matter of integrity. This is the question: Is what we are when we are alone by ourselves the same as when we are gathered with others, whether the group is two or three or if it is two or three hundred? If we are, whether in public or in private, we can be sure that God is with us.

---

1   Tom Wright, *Matthew for Everyone Part 1*, SPCK, London 2002, p 56.

CHAPTER 7
FINDING A WELCOME

Matthew 10:5-15

I recently retired after forty years of active pastoral service. An interesting thing happened on the way to church. After being in church all those years, my wife, Susan, and I woke up that first Sunday morning and realized that we had nowhere to go to church. We were church homeless. At least for the time being, we did not have a church home. It was the first time in my professional life that I did not know where I was going to go to worship on Sunday.

During this first year of retirement, we spent our Sunday mornings visiting churches we knew and some that we had only heard about. At last count, we mostly showed up unexpectedly in about sixteen different congregations, ranging from high church Roman Catholic to low church Unitarian-Universalist, from African-American gospel to suburbanite megachurch. But whatever the type of church, the same question was always in the back of our minds: Would we find a welcome there?

This question had a way of taking several forms. Will we be comfortable there? Will they make us feel at home, at least for the moment? Who's going to be there? What kind of people are they? Will we know anybody there?

Obviously, in some cases we felt at home because we already knew someone in the congregation. In fact, in some instances we had already received an invitation to visit before we arrived. It was a joy to see a friendly face. And on the whole, I have to say, that while we were warmly greeted in almost all instances, some congregations are more adept at the ministry of hospitality than others.

In the larger sense, our year-long tour of churches caused me to ponder what it means to find a welcome in a congregation. My baseline is the same as for many. The congregation I grew up in sixty years ago still serves as the standard by which I find myself measuring other congregations. It was in my home congregation that I came to love church. These were the people of God who gave me both roots and wings, as they say. Roots to provide a heritage and soil to grow in. Wings to try out my talents and develop my skills, stumble and fall and get up and take another go at it. It was in my home congregation in Kentucky that I first heard Jesus' words of forgiveness, about what it means to forgive not seven times, but seventy times seven. Later there would be other churches in college and in divinity school and throughout my professional life as a minister that would serve as my "church home." But it was still my home congregation that set the standard by which I measured all of these. And not only for me, but for my wife and our children as well. The congregations we served in Indiana not only provided my wife and me with a friendly environment, but also demonstrated how preachers' kids can "find a welcome in the Shepherd's flock and fold."[1]

Now this is not always the case. As a pastor, I've talked to many prospective members who have not found it so in the congregations they are leaving. Some have shared stories about how they were terrorized by certain individuals in a particular congregation. Others have related how they never felt they fit in. But as I listened to these stories, what was amazing to me was that it was not my experience. More often than not, as we were vacationing and traveling, our family found a welcoming presence in the congregations we visited. Of course, it helped whenever they learned that we were a visiting pastor and wife.

Yet, sadly there are times when anyone, anywhere, even a minister, can experience anything but a glad reception in the church. As a young pastor, I learned the hard way that it's better not to go to *any* New Year's party hosted by a member in the congregation than to go to two parties. It just doesn't work to try to please everyone by leaving one party early and arriving at another late. I found myself the victim of "Well, if you'd rather be with them than us.

---

1   Fred Pratt Green, "God Is Here," *Words*.

That's OK." That's one New Year's Eve I've never forgotten, and probably why to this day New Year's Eve is not one of my favorite holidays. But that poor judgment and hurtful experience aside, there have not been many places where I have not felt welcome, even in places outside the church. In fact, I can count them on the fingers of my hand. I don't feel welcome at rock concerts, they're too loud. Or to places that cater only to the college age, I'm too old. But as I look around me, obviously those who are happy there way out number me.

But before we go on too long with this, maybe we had better check in with what the New Testament says about it, and particularly with some of the things Jesus himself had to say about finding a welcome and extending one. According to Jesus, where should we expect to be received warmly?

In Matthew's account, as Jesus is sending the twelve disciples out on their first mission, preaching and teaching, he gives this sage advice: "Whatever town or village you enter, find out who in it is worthy, and stay there until you leave." In other words, go first to those you suspect will welcome you. Go to the "worthy." And who are these? They are where the gospel has already been planted and taken root.

Most churches I know say "All Are Welcome." But in fact, not all are. On the surface, it may appear to be that way. But it takes a while to find out that all is not as it appears. One of my saddest moments as a pastor was what a couple of young women--who from all appearances were just that, a committed couple–said to me. As I was trying to explain to them how I thought they might experience our congregation as it struggled with the gay issue, I heard them say to me, "Then you're not as open as we thought. You're just like all other Christian churches." I assured them that we were not like the other congregations they had encountered. I was only trying to be honest. I was trying to tell them that I thought they might run upon some obstacles in our community life. The sad thing was, they had done what Jesus advised. They had gone to the place where they felt they would be accepted. And they had been. But they just didn't even want to entertain the possibility that not everyone in the church would feel the same way about them.

The next thing Jesus says is that we should stick it out for a while to see what happens. That's personally where I think these two young women went astray. They were not willing to do as others like them since have done. Jesus may have even had another reason for what he said. When he told the disciples not to leave the house that had welcomed them, he may have simply been telling them not to shop around to see if they could find something better, perhaps a better B&B, with more comfortable sleeping arrangements and a bigger breakfast bar. No, they were to stick it out for as long as they were there. They were to go home "with the one that brung them to the dance." An elder I knew used to tell the students in his high school church school class, "When you go to college, be sure to attend church and sit in the same pew for three Sundays in a row. By then, someone will have to say hello to you."

Furthermore, these itinerant disciples of Jesus were not only to reside with this host family, but bless it. They are to "let their peace come upon it." They are to bless as they have been blessed. There's more to it than just being a good house guest. They are to be a blessing to the house. They are to grace them with their presence. Haven't we all had people stay in our home who made us feel better than before they came? They left us with more of a blessing than we gave to them, or at least as much. We couldn't wait until they could come back for a visit. I think that's what Jesus is trying to say.

Then if it doesn't work, move on. In Jesus' words, "let your peace return to you. If anyone will not welcome you or listen to your words, shake off the dust from your feet as you leave that house or town." Sometimes we just have to realize that it's not going to work out.

After about six months of visiting churches, Susan and I realized that we couldn't go on doing this forever. And like many others have found, we finally had to take into consideration one deciding factor in determining where we would go to church. It is not the only factor to be sure, but it is, perhaps, the main one: Where did WE feel most welcome?

And how did this come about? How did these congregations do it? How did these particular congregations make us feel welcome? Of the congregations we visited, one thing stood out. It's just like Jesus told his disciples when he sent them out. We felt most welcome when we went to a place where we were already known. Being introduced, affirmed, even our presence acknowledged publicly, of course, had something to do with it. It's nice to be known. Viewed from this perspective, I now know even better why church growth experts say that upwards to 80 percent of first-time visitors to a worship service are there because someone in the congregation invited them. It some ways it's a scary proposition to walk into an unfamiliar congregation unless you've been brought there or are invited by someone you know and trust. I now have my own personal proof of why growing churches are so intentional about urging their members to invite their friends to church. It's what works best. Knowing that there will be someone there we know when we enter the door, qualms a lot of fears that we may have about attending a particular congregation for the first time.

Then we also took Jesus' second word to heart. We stuck it out. We went back several times to these particular congregations, and found that our welcome grew. That's how they did it. That's how these particular congregations made us feel at home.

But it can happen in a most unlikely and perhaps unknown place as well. We were attending Evensong at King's College Chapel in Cambridge, England. At one of these gatherings the congregation is made up of people of all nationalities and beliefs, with people sitting side-by-side to many of whom will likely never see each other again. Yet all are there for the same dual purpose, to see this magnificent building and to hear this outstanding choir. On this occasion when we were visiting, moments before the service, a woman in the congregation began to cough incessantly. Her cough could be heard bouncing around the limestone walls and reverberating from the Gothic ceiling throughout that historic building. As the choir was lining up to process and it was almost time for them to sing, I thought to myself, what others present must have been thinking as well, "Why doesn't this woman just get up and get a drink and leave the rest of us in peace to listen to these heavenly voices?" As I was getting more and more agitated, the Dean of the Chapel walked over to the lectern, picked up a glass of water, and proceeded down the center aisle to this lady to give her a drink. Jesus' words "a cup of cold water" never took on so much meaning for me as at that moment. In giving that lady a drink of water, the good Dean not only ministered to her, but to all the hundreds who were anticipating meeting God through the marvelous voices of the choir. I wouldn't be surprised that in that instant everyone present felt they had found a welcome.

CHAPTER 8

SERPENTS AND DOVES

Matthew 10:16-23

Jesus said that we are to be as wise as serpents and as innocent as doves. But sometimes we are neither. Even in little things.

One Christmas, my wife and I were having a party for the church staff, something we both liked to do each year. Since I love to cook, I enjoy sharing in the meal preparations. This particular Christmas, things were even more hectic than usual. The guests were arriving. We were busy hurrying around, trying to beat the clock. In a mad rush, I put a tray of rolls on the bottom rack of the oven. Ten minutes later, as I was pulling them out, the organist at the church, herself a master chef, was looking over my shoulder. When she saw what I had done, and where I had placed the pan of rolls in the oven, she remarked, "That looks dangerous to me. I'm not bold enough to try that." Well, as could be expected, the rolls were all rightly burned on the bottom. I immediately said to my musical friend, "Yes, you're right. There is no excuse for what I did. It's nothing less than a sin. I knew better." She laughed. But in that moment, I realized that even in the little things of life, Jesus is right. In placing that pan of rolls on the bottom rack of the oven, I was being neither wise nor innocent.

But where is the sin in that? No one was really hurt, were they? But I was, and all those rolls with their burned bottoms resulted in there being fewer rolls to go around. Rather than making more wine for the feast as Jesus did on that day at a wedding in Cana of Galilee, I contributed to making our celebration of his birth a little less abundant.

It can be more personal than this. I'm thinking of all those things we eat and drink that are not good for us. Right after I had prostate cancer surgery, I was given some information to read about follow-up procedures. One piece of advice stuck vividly in my imagination. "If following this surgery, you decide to go out drinking with the guys, you deserve whatever happens to you." A wise word indeed.

More often than not, it's more like having a cup of real tea in the afternoon or regular coffee at dinner, or God forbid, chocolate ice cream right before going to bed. I know these are a "no-no" for me at my age. My hiatal hernia and acid reflux don't like being mistreated like that. But on occasion after occasion, it seems that I have to learn the lesson over again. For some strange reason, I like to test the waters and see if perhaps I can get by with it this time. And at those times, I usually find myself getting up in the wee hours of the morning in search of an antacid. What I had decided to do was neither wise nor innocent. Wishing it so does not make it so. Once again, I find out the hard way that I am neither a serpent nor a dove; I'm a louse.

In the bigger issues of life, this approach can prove devastating for everyone far and near. It's still not entirely clear whether the US government was wise or innocent in the response to Hurricane Katrina. Initially, the delayed response in the coastal disaster appeared to be a lack of knowing how to handle such a massive natural occurrences on our own shores. We were caught off guard, it was said. But then we learned that there had been warnings for some time from those who were in the know; it was only a matter of time before something like this would happen. But even with this prior knowledge, no action was taken. Things went on as usual, like the proverbial ostrich sticking its head in the sand. Neither wise nor innocent. How sad when those involved lost everything they had, including someone they loved, while the rest of us ended up paying higher prices for everything from PCP pipe to gasoline. Today, are we any wiser? Any less innocent?

Mencken: The American Iconoclast by Marion Elizabeth Rodgers is a fascinating biography of H. L. Mencken, the famous journalist of a previous generation. He was known by millions for the stinging, vitriolic way he put his points across. His penchant for pithy sayings and aphorisms still has a way of entrancing us all. Everyone knows what Mencken means when he says that "A Puritan is someone who cannot rest as long as he thinks there might be some person somewhere on earth that might be happy." Or this one: "No one in the world ever lost money by underestimating the intelligence of the great masses of the plain people." With time now on our side, it appears that Mencken may have been the one person around at the time who knew what was going on, at least on several controversial issues. Mencken is often referred to as a wise man of letters, maybe one of the wisest. But his hard-driving lifestyle of cigar smoking, liquor swigging, and womanizing could not by any measure be called innocent. In fact, his personal life gave him the nickname of "The Bad Boy of Baltimore." His perspective on American life, viewed from the unique vantage point of being born into a German immigrant family living on the Eastern seaboard, has given him a credibility in the newspaper business that has lasted beyond his day. But it was not always appreciated at the time. Mencken's observations of life still ring true. We still see the world being run for the wrong reasons. We continue to rely on policies that are meant mainly to justify the needs and ideology of the powerful. Very wise insights by not such an innocent man.

Baba, the father of Amir, the main character, in Khaled Hosseini's best-selling novel, *The Kite Runner*, comes across as a high powered, businessman, but with lofty ideals and goals. After all, Baba did at one time found an orphanage for unwanted children. As time progressed, Baba's native land of Afghanistan was overrun by the Taliban. Finally, Baba was forced to leave for America with his son. As the novel unfolds, the reader, as well as his son learns about decisions his father made that compromised his innocence and integrity. Wise, Baba may have been, but innocent he was not. Baba was certainly not the doting father his son at one time believed him to be.

Then some of us have another problem. We are innocent, but not wise. This is precisely the problem many ministers have. They mean well, but don't always know what they're doing. While learning how to become a pastor in Detroit, theologian Reinhold

Niebuhr discovered the main reason that many ministers are less than prophetic in the pulpit. Niebuhr observed that many times pastors do not speak out, not because they are cowards, but because they are too tender-hearted. Most pastors do not want to hurt the people they are preaching to. They have come to love these people as they have ministered to them in times of crisis. It's the minister's pastoral heart that works against their prophetic presence in the pulpit.

Of course, where all this really matters is on the larger scale of things. Think of suicide bombers and terrorists. Most of us do not pretend to understand the psychological makeup of this kind of person. It is hard to put ourselves in their place. There is reason to believe that this kind of terrorist must stem from a condition that breeds innocence, but not wisdom.

In his novel, *The Terrorist*, John Updike is able to do what many of us cannot. Updike has an uncanny ability to put himself in the shoes of a potential young terrorist by the name of Ahmad. This young man is of divorced parents. His father was Egyptian, his mother American. Because of this, Ahmad grew up in the U.S. in a religious vacuum. His father was absent. His mother was a free thinker of the love-child generation. She had a high-minded, but misguided view that her son could decide on a religion when he grew up. Longing for his missing father, Ahmad falls into the eager hands of an imam, the leader of the local mosque. However, this leader also turns out not only to be a devout teacher, but the head of a suicide bombing operation. Ahmad is a faithful student of the Qur'an, extremely naive, and vulnerable to the mesmerizing influence of the misguided Islamic cleric. The novel is a touching picture of the development of a true-believer, one who is, for all purposes, naive to the point of manipulation, lacking in perspective to make sense out of what he's being taught and, even more, of what he's going through. Innocence without wisdom is a dangerous combination. It's just waiting for someone to come along and ignite wrong-headed thinking with deep passion. In a word, innocent, but not wise.

So where does this leave us? Maybe with a greater appreciation of what Jesus meant when he told his disciples that he was sending them out like sheep in the midst of wolves. They were to be wise as serpents and innocent as doves.

This teaching takes place following the sending out of the twelve. Most New Testament scholars think that this passage in Matthew has as much to say about what was going on in the life of the church in the writer's day as it does about what Jesus intended in his day. (Interestingly, this verse is found only in Matthew's gospel; yet the Gospel of Thomas knows this verse.)

The contrast is meant to be dramatic. Doves are innocent creatures, not birds of prey. Snakes, on the other hand, have been suspect from the Garden of Eden. Jesus' point is that we are to be both wise and innocent. The goal is to strike a balance between the two. No easy trick.

It doesn't take too much living in this world to discern that just surviving requires a certain amount of shrewdness. Rabbis used this saying in teaching Israel how to deal with Gentiles. In Matthew's gospel, now the concern is with how the early Christians are to deal with their Jewish brothers and sisters who are becoming more and more hostile to the newly growing Christian gospel. As it comes to us in Matthew, the verse offers guidance about how Christians are to behave in times of persecution.

If there is a word to describe how we are to go about it, it would be that antique word *prudence*. According to Matthew, conditions are getting worse for the Jewish Christians in the local synagogues. There are even reports that some of these early Christians are being persecuted. Matthew does not supply us with the exact details as to why they are being flogged. It seems to have to do with the tensions the early Christians are experiencing as they try to be faithful to Jesus' mission. Whatever happens to them, they are to remain faithful to the truth they have learned in Jesus. They are to remain steadfast even when handed over to the authorities. Reading between the lines, the goal is for the early disciples to imitate Jesus and undergo sufferings in the way he did. At all times, they are to follow the leading of the Holy Spirit. The only guidelines they will receive are the words that the Holy Spirit will give them. Interestingly, in these verses from Matthew, these early Christians are not told how to defend themselves. That is not the main concern. Even in these dire circumstances, the emphasis is on how to proclaim the gospel. Yet, it must have come as a comfort to know that when the pressure was on, through the guidance of the Spirit, they would know what to say and do.

Not to compare my personal ministerial experience with that of the early disciples, I do recall a time when I was under pressure as a senior minister of a congregation. We were in the process of calling an additional staff member. The pressure came during a board meeting that was called to take action on a candidate. As the meeting progressed, I found myself saying words that surely only the Holy Spirit could have provided.

It all had to do with the employment of a recently divorced minister as our associate minister. This all took place some thirty-five years ago, when matters such as this were more unusual than they are now. I was certain that this person was the right person for the job. And even more important, I was convinced that this was the Christian thing to do. We were being given the opportunity to give this young minister a break and open the doors of Christian ministry to him, so that he could use the gifts and graces with which God had abundantly equipped him.

I remember vividly the moment an elder emeritus stood up and looked me straight in the face and said, "Preacher, do you mean to tell me that you are recommending that we hire a divorced man to serve our church?" I said, "That's exactly what I'm saying." He replied, "If he's as good as you say he is, will you guarantee that he will not cause our church any trouble?" Then in a moment, in the twinkling of an eye, I found myself saying: "No, I can't do that. For that matter, I won't even guarantee that you will not cause our church any trouble." I thought to myself, "Well, now, David, you've done it. Better go home and pack your bags." There was a silence in the room, which felt to me like that half hour silence the book of Revelation mentions. Then this elderly gentleman chuckled, and began to laugh out loud. "Smart man, our preacher. If I had a vote, I would vote for the divorced man the minister wants as our associate." And then he sat down. That's what I think about every time I hear these words of Jesus telling all of us Christians that we are to be as wise as serpents and as meek as doves. As it turned out, the congregation did call that ministerial candidate, and that person provided an excellent ministry for our church and for the denomination.

Oxford professor R. T. France has put it quite well. "The balance of prudence and purity will enable Christians both to survive and to fulfill their mission in the world."[1] Looked at this way, we can begin to see why Jesus told his disciples that when they were persecuted in one town they were to flee to the next. The practical advice to "get out while the getting is good" amounts to simply not being stupid. In times of persecution, it simply doesn't make sense to take unnecessary risks. It's just not worth it to stand up and fight a losing cause. Even Jesus himself backed off from confrontation at times. That is, until his hour had come. And then Jesus voluntarily submitted himself to what had to be, knowing in his heart that he was doing God's will. Like Jesus, the only thing we can be certain of is that we will never know in advance what to do. Only at the time will it all become clear. "Shrewd, but guileless" is another way it has been described.[2]

Tom Wright, Bishop of Durham, has a clear, but elegant way of summing things up. Wright says, "Without innocence shrewdness becomes manipulation; without shrewdness innocence becomes naivety. Though we face different crises and different problems to those of the first disciples, we still need that finely balanced character, reflecting so remarkably that of Jesus himself."[3]

What, then, are we to be? Serpents? Doves? Wise? Innocent? Or both? Yes. "Let those with ears, hear."

---

1   T. France, *Matthew*, Leicester, UK: Inter-Varsity Press 1985, p 182.

2   Daniel J. Harrington, *The Gospel According to Matthew*, Collegeville Bible Commentary, Collegeville, Minnesota: The Liturgical Press 1983, p 47.

3   Tom Wright, *Matthew for Everyone*, London: SPCK 2002, p 117.

CHAPTER 9

THAT AWE-FULL EXCHANGE RATE!

Matthew 10:38-39, Mark 8:34-37, Luke 9:23-26, John 12:25-26

One of the first things you notice when you travel from the U.S. to Britain these days is how expensive things are "over there." At first glance, it does not seem so bad. A medium value meal at Burger King is 3.99 pounds. A bit pricey. Then you realize that, in U.S. currency, that's almost $8.00. Pricey, indeed! And to make matters worse, most meals in England are considerably more expensive than that.

And then there's the matter of petrol, or gasoline. When I was on sabbatical in England in 2004, gasoline was about 84 pence per litre. That's about $8.00 a gallon. And we think we have it bad!

When it comes to owning a home, that's a major undertaking for most Brits these days. An average detached home, that is, one on its own lot, can run anywhere from 80,000 to 150,000 pounds, or about $160,000 to $300.000.

Of course, much of the problem is that awful exchange rate. As I write, the British pound is almost double the American dollar. The rate of exchange makes us aware of what economists refer to as "comparative value." In plain words, "This is what you get for that." Since a U.S. dollar is worth so little now in comparison with the British pound, Brits love to travel to New York City and to Disney World. It's relatively cheap for them. Their money goes much further in the US because the English pound is so strong against the American dollar.

Understanding the dynamics of the exchange rate and the concept of comparative value is a good way to understand some of the paradoxical sayings of Jesus. The parallel scripture passage in Matthew 10 is almost identical to the one in Mark 8. In his commentary on Matthew, Walter Davies reminds us that Jesus was fond of riddles and paradoxes. If so, the saying about losing one's life to save it is the ultimate paradox. A helpful way to understand the saying is to look at it in the way of comparative value. In other words, what's the exchange rate for the eternal life preached by Jesus worth?[1] In Matthew's way of thinking, if you believe this and do that, this is what you can expect.

Mark, the earliest gospel account, puts it like this:

> He (Jesus) called the crowd with his disciples, and said to them, "If any want to become my followers, let them deny themselves and take up their cross, and follow me. For those who want to save their life will lose it, and those who lose their life for my sake, and for the sake of the gospel, will save it. For what will it profit them to gain the whole world and forfeit their life? Indeed, what can they give in return for their life?"

There are not many things that can be harder for most of us than to put ourselves last and God first. But that's the kind of exchange Jesus is asking for. For most of us, most of the time, that rate is just too high. We're not sure it's a good deal. It's hard to put Number One aside while you're trying to look out for Number One at the same time. And yet, isn't that what modern life seems to require? We hear it all the time. "If you don't look out for yourself, who will?"

What's being asked of us in exchange for the good life is an encompassing list. It includes things like privilege, advantage, reputation, comfort, and respect, and at times, even dying for the cause of Christ. Certainly, that has been true in times past. Jesus says that to cling to these things is to give up authentic life for a

---

1   W.D. Davies and Dale C. Allison Jr., *Matthew Vol 2*, Edinburgh : T&T Clark 1991, p 79.

false one. No wonder he warned that the gate is narrow, and few there are who enter it.

These are hard demands. They are not just about giving up something for Lent, like ice cream or chocolate. It requires putting our self interest aside in exchange for a life of service to God and neighbour. "Anyone who wishes to be a follower of mine, he must leave self behind," says Jesus. But this hard saying is followed by an even harder one. "... he must take up his cross, and come with me." (NEB)

In a day of cheap grace and a gospel of health, wealth and prosperity, these sayings of Jesus sound almost unbelievable, certainly unattainable, utterly beyond the reach of ordinary human beings. There is no yellow brick road leading us to the Emerald City. Jesus tells us that unless we go down this rocky, hard road, we will never reach the Eternal City.

Matthew's account doesn't make it any easier than Mark's. Matthew prefaces these words of Jesus with even stronger ones.

> Whoever loves father or mother more than me is not worthy of me; and whoever loves son or daughter more than me is not worthy of me; and whoever does not take up the cross and follow me is not worthy of me. Those who find their life will lose it; and those who lose their life for my sake will find it.

The cross we are to bear is made up of all of those obstacles on the road of life that get in the way of our following Jesus. These obstacles are many and varied, and different for each of us. Yet even though the obstacles are different, they all probably revolve around a few that we have in common: work, play, family, and maybe even our church activities. It can be whatever causes us to stumble as we try to follow Jesus' way of life of love and service.

These requirements are so severe that many of us often try to find a way around them. Like W.C. Fields, we read the Bible hoping to find a loophole. We trick ourselves into believing that these demands were only meant for the original disciples. We convince ourselves that we do not have to worry about keeping them today. But there's nothing in these passages to suggest that these demands of Jesus are to be restricted in any way, to anyone, whatsoever. The requirements for entrance to the kingdom of God are the same for any and all who want to join up at any time.

I suppose it all comes down to a matter of priorities, as we like to say these days. And so it does. These are the questions that nag us to death: If I do this for you, what will I get? What's in it for me? Spiritually speaking, what's the current exchange rate to follow Jesus? And the answer? Like the current exchange rate between the US and Britain, it may not be one we want to hear. Jesus tells us that the exchange rate for following him is all or nothing.

In a way, the saying in John's gospel is the most difficult of all. In John 12:25 we read "Those who love their life lose it, and those who *hate* their life in this world will keep it for eternal life." To me, hating life reeks of an unhealthy self-loathing, the kind of low self-esteem we ministers advise people to go to a counsellor or psychiatrist to get rid of. But still, when we put this kind of language aside, the basic point in John is the same. Regardless of the words being used, the gospel message is the same. We have to put self aside if we are ever to find anything resembling a life of satisfaction for ourselves, much less to be of encouragement for others. The same paradoxical exchange is asked for. "Whoever seeks to save his life will lose it, whoever loses his life will save it."

The way Luke records this saying is in some ways easier and in other ways more difficult to accept. "If any want to become my followers, let them deny themselves and take up their cross daily and follow me." Now Luke tells us that it's not just a one time affair. It's not just, "Bite the bullet and get it over with." It's not, as my doctor told me, "Have that back surgery so you can go to England pain free."

Luke has a way of always bringing things down to the here and now. Luke tells us that it's something we have to do *daily*. We can't just get it over with once and for all. There will be no time in our lives when we will NOT have to deny ourselves, NOT have to take up our cross, NOT have to follow Jesus. We have to do it all the time, day in and day out. No wonder Martin Luther spoke of it as "a daily baptism." For so it is. Each day we have to begin anew. Better yet, each day we *get* to begin again. And some days we may even have to (or get to) begin more than once. Each day we are called to put ourselves aside and do what needs to be done. The show must go on, no matter how sick we are, no matter how ill prepared we may be. Hard sayings indeed! Yet the promise is that when we do, the exchange rate is way in our favor. But make no mistake about it. Clearly, what Jesus is urging us to do is often directly opposed to much of modern day life.

Also, while on sabbatical in England, I ran upon an encouraging newspaper interview with novelist John Updike in the *The Guardian*. Updike is one of my favorite authors. I love the way he describes things, especially the way he chronicles the period of American life he's writing about. Updike was in Britain at the time of the interview because he was being honored at the Guardian Hay Festival. The newspaper article seemed to suggest that he was the greatest American writer alive. However, not many people in America or in the UK may know what a committed Christian Updike is. He's one of a very few modern novelists who is self-consciously and intentionally committed to the Christian faith. Besides that, Updike is an active member of his church. In the newspaper article, Updike put his finger on a modern problem. He said that in so much of life today we act like nothing very much matters. One thing is as good as another. What attracts him to the Christian faith is that it tells him that some things *do* matter, and some more than others.

Updike practices what he preaches. There was a time when he was called to leave his home in Vermont and come to New York City to receive an important honor. When Updike found out the date of the event, and that it was to be on a Sunday, he said, "I can't be there. I've promised to teach the Junior High Sunday School Class all this summer. If you want me, it will have to be on a day other than Sunday." Of course, many good Christians might make a case that the famous author could have gotten a substitute to teach the class and accepted the invitation without so much as a second thought. But that was not the point. Updike had made a commitment to those youth and to God to be there in person. And that was more important than any other honor he himself might be given. If a person like John Updike can turn down a fancy award dinner in New York City in his honor, because he thinks teaching junior high boys and girls about Jesus is more important, what does that say about him? More importantly, what does it say about the rest of us? For my money, I say, Updike's heart is in the right place. And maybe the rest of us need to examine how well we're doing at denying ourselves and carrying our crosses, day in and day out.

If I had to put what I'm trying to say in a nut shell, it comes down to asking ourselves if we have not become "a bit too casual" in our commitment to Christianity. I am reminded of a comment about a certain bishop of whom it was said, "He had recurring bouts with Christianity. But he usually got over them."

The call of Jesus is one of urgency. And it runs crashing head long into the modern day habit of leaving our options open. "Try to take everything as it comes," we say, as if one thing is as good as another, and nothing much matters anyway. After all, "tomorrow is another day." The Jesus of the gospels will have none of this. He tells us that whether we like it or not, there is a deadline on our lives. Today may be the only day we have to set things right. So the question: "What will it profit them to gain the whole world and forfeit their own life? Indeed, what can they give in return for their life?" And the answer? Absolutely nothing, nothing whatsoever.

But looked at the other way around, those who lose their life for the sake of Christ and the gospel will find it. That's a very good rate of exchange, if you ask me. But don't ask me, ask Jesus! He will tell you about another exchange rate, that Awe-full exchange rate. One that is full of grace and truth, the exchange rate of the Kingdom of God.

CHAPTER 10

TO COMFORT, TO CHALLENGE, TO LEARN

Matthew 11:28-30, Matthew 16:24

Why do we go to church? Is it out of, "custom," as Luke said about Jesus, who went to the synagogue regularly? Or does someone make us go, like our mother or father, or our wife or husband, maybe even a girlfriend or boyfriend? Or do we go for one of the best reasons of all, someone invited us to go, for they wanted us to find what they have found in church? Is that the reason? Or do we go all by ourselves hoping to find God, yearning to make a connection with the sustaining power of the universe, and we thought that this might just be the place? All of these are possible reasons why we *might* find ourselves in church.

But underneath all of these, on any given Sunday, there are possibly three other reasons why many people attend worship. When we come to church, we come with differing expectations and needs.

Some come to find comfort; they need to have a burden lifted. Some come to be challenged; they need to be motivated to live life more fully than they may be right now.

Still others come out of a yearning to learn a little more about Jesus; they hope to find a spiritual lesson that will get them through the week.

As a pastor usually chosen to speak to these concerns week after week, the question may take this form: How can any preacher speak to all of these needs on any given Sunday? In truth, it's impossible. The best that most preachers can accomplish is to meet one or two of these concerns. But, then, two out of three ain't all that bad.

What the preacher can do is to attempt to keep some kind of balance among these three needs. Throughout the year, sermons can be planned to address each of these needs. That's what some ministers try to do throughout their ministries. While they may not always be successful, it may mean that some of the time the accent is stronger on one concern than the other. But that's the goal. And since people have a way of showing up in worship every so often, even the best preaching plan can be altered by the fact that on any given Sunday, the message that a particular person needs to hear might have been given on one of the Sundays when they were not in attendance.

As a preacher, I became acutely aware of this some time ago. The concern actually reflects the paradoxical teaching style of Jesus. For me, it all began during a weekend at a Catholic retreat center. The leader was a Christian psychotherapist. She possessed a beautiful, Christian spirit. She was one of the most transparent persons to God's love in Christ that I'd ever met.

As a part of the weekend, this adept leader had each participant decide which one of three groups they needed to be in. There was a group for "rest," another for "go," and one for "learn." Each small group was based on one of the three sayings of Jesus in Matthew, Chapters 11 and 16.

As a part of this retreat, I chose the rest group. I felt that was the word I needed to hear at that time in my life. But what transpired was not what I was expecting. Rather than let each of us tell about how tired we were, the leader proceeded to tell us about a time in her life when she was completely, physically, emotionally, and spiritually exhausted. She went into detail about how she had given her life to serving Christ and the church to the point that she was literally immobilized in bed. She could not even turn herself over. She was so spent. She had to have someone come in and do that for her. Now, I must say I've been tired, but I have never been that tired. After serving as a counselor for a couple of weeks 24/7 in a private camp for elementary age children, I once slept fifteen hours straight, but even then, I could still manage to get out of bed on my own. Listening to this leader relate her personal condition had a surprising effect on me. I felt my own burden being lifted and my tiredness passing away. My heart went out to her. I was sorry that the other two groups who chose other leaders did not get to hear her story. I think they missed out on a wonderful testimony about what it means to serve God and not burn yourself out in the process. But from all the reports, those who chose to "go" and those who decided to "learn," seemed to have gotten just as much out of their experiences with their leaders as I did with mine. Perhaps, it was because they were ready to move on or dig deeper into something they wanted to know more about than I was at that moment.

There is a word of caution before we look further into each of these three modes of the Christian life. Before we try to see where we might be, I want to warn that it's possible to trick ourselves about what we really need and feel. It is possible that we can be so out of touch with our own needs and feelings that we might even sign up for the wrong workshop. It is possible to think that we need to rest, when what we really need is to go. Or we may think we need to learn, when what we actually need is to rest.

It is said that the renowned psychiatrist, Karl Menninger, used to surprise people in the way he went about treating patients with depression. Rather than initially spending time with them and giving them advice and comfort, Dr. Menninger would often put the patients to physical work, such as chopping wood. He found that many times depressed patients need to get back in touch with their physical bodies before any successful therapy can take place in their minds and spirits. Likewise, with those who love to read and study, who are always looking for that next book that will solve all their problems, sometimes the last thing they need is to read. They may need to rest or to go visit someone who needs cheering up.

I had a professor who told me thirty-five years ago, "David, you have a gift for writing, but you will never write, if you do not stop reading." Only now at this stage in my life am I beginning to heed his good counsel.

And so it goes with those who are always more than ready to do something for Jesus. They might just be more tired than they know. But they never stop long enough to realize that they need to rest.

The goal is for each person to get in touch with their inner feelings and deepest needs, so that they can let the gospel speak to them. We might also take to heart the wise counsel Martin Luther once gave to his students when they complained that they couldn't understand a certain Bible verse. Luther's advice was, "If you can't understand the passage, it's not meant for you right now. Go on to another passage that you do understand, and then come back to the troubling passage later. In time, it will speak to you when you're ready to hear it." Good advice.

So what you we need to hear today? A word of comfort? A word of challenge? A word of truth?

What about a word of comfort? This is exactly what many people find they need. One morning, as a pastor, I was making phone calls trying to get various individuals to do what they had said they would do in the church, I was struck by the answers I received during those phone calls. One after another told me why they hadn't been able to get around to their duties. One leader I talked to said that they were down with the flu. Still another had received word of a death in the family. Still another had a problem with a teenager that was driving them crazy. Still another was trying to sell their house, and another had just received a job offer in another community. When I hung up the phone, I thought to myself, "No wonder the church of Jesus Christ is not moving like a mighty army. The troops are sick!" Everyone I talked with that morning needed a word of comfort. They desperately needed to hear Jesus words, "Come to me, all you that are weary and are carrying heavy burdens, and I will give you rest."

Pastors who are also called to be administrators have a constant concern as to how they are to minister to the needs of hurting individuals and also take care of the needs of the church at large. It's even harder when the troops are sick.

Jesus says, "Take my yoke upon you." A yoke is a device put on animals so that they can carry something that they might otherwise not be able to. A yoke is designed to make carrying the burden easier and lighter. Using this image, Jesus was very hard on the religious leaders of his day. He said that they were doing the very opposite. They were guilty of making things worse for their people not better.

Interestingly, Jesus' solution is not to get rid of the yoke, but to take on a different one. Jesus offered a different yoke. One of the best sermons I ever heard was preached one morning in chapel during my stay at divinity school. The preacher for the day preached an outstanding sermon on these verses from Matthew. As with all good sermons, the preacher left each of us with a question to sort out for ourselves. He looked us straight in the eye and said, "If the burden you are carrying for the Lord is heavy, could it be that it's not the Lord's burden that you are carrying, but one of your own making? Jesus says his yoke is easy and his burden is light."

To find rest is not to be released from all obligations, but to find the service that is invigorating to you personally. We all know what it feels like to be tired from doing something that we have to do that we would rather not do. It's draining. It's debilitating. It's the difference between a heavy load and a light one. It's the difference between a yoke that has been polished smooth and one left rough and raw to irritate the animal's skin. It's the same feeling one might get from wearing a piece of wool straight off the sheep's back and that which has been processed to a fine finish.

What about a word of challenge? Is that what you need to hear today? Tom Wright translates Jesus' words this way: "If anyone wants to come after me, they must give themselves up, pick up their cross, and follow me."[1] This is without a doubt the most difficult demand than can be asked of anyone. I know it is for most of us Americans. Even the best of us are afflicted with accumulating things. We are good at taking things on, not giving them up.

It's true even with good things. When I began my ministry, I eagerly looked forward to the day when I would have a nice study filled with books from floor to ceiling. Well, when I retired

1   Tom Wright, *Matthew for Everyone*, London: SPCK 2002, p 9.

after forty years of service, I had it, but also the daunting task of culling all those books down to the space we could find at home. Even purchasing three new bookcases wouldn't do it. The shelves at home rapidly filled to capacity. If once I had thought that following Christ meant to have a lot of books, now I found they had become an obstacle. For I now found it very difficult to part with any of them, or at least most of them.

Granted, it was not books that Jesus had in mind for his disciples, but people. Special people. Jesus told them that if they followed him, they might be called upon to put their service to him above their own families. That's what it might mean to come and follow him, given the way things were back then. The cross is the ultimate symbol of self-denial. And to break with family, would certainly be taking up one's cross. I particularly like the way a commentary on these verses puts it. "Jesus is talking about the willingness to give up personal ambition, even suffer, die for God's cause."[1]

The call of Jesus has been compared to a bell in a distant church that keeps calling us from whatever we may be doing. It's as if every time the bell tolls, we hear it saying to us, "pick up your cross and follow me, pick up your cross and follow me." The sound resonates throughout the town and into the stores and offices, school rooms and hospital beds. "Pick up your cross and follow me."[2] Is that the word we need to hear today?

Then what about a word of truth? Do we need to learn more about Jesus today? Jesus said, "Take my yoke upon you and learn from me; for I am gentle and humble in heart; and you will find rest for your soul. For my yoke is easy, and my burden is light." Easy can mean good as well as kind, rather than not difficult or demanding.

I suspect that members of the Christian Church (Disciples of Christ) are most at home learning about the truths of God. After all, the very word, disciple, means student or learner. And it's no secret that many Disciples have an insatiable desire to learn

---

1   W.D. Davies and Dale C. Allison Jr., *Matthew Vol. 2*, Edinburgh: T&T Clark, 1991, p 671

2   Tom Wright, *Matthew for Everyone*, London: SPCK 2002, p 11

more about God. For myself, I came by this honestly. The minister who had the most influence on me was a devoted student of the Bible. My divinity school has a motto, *Lux et veritas* (Light and Truth.) But it also has two unwritten mottoes. Motto one: "Look at everything in the best possible light." Motto two: "Always try to advance the discussion." To this day, I'm very concerned if I feel that I have not left those who listen to my preaching with a fresh word on the subject.

But what Jesus is getting at is not more words *about* him, but a personal relationship *with* him. You see, it's the teacher that matters. Hopefully, most of us have had a teacher that we would have done anything for just because the teacher was that kind of a teacher. My high school band director was that kind of a teacher. He could get anyone to do anything for him. He also happened to be the choir director at my home church. One Sunday morning, during my freshman year, he tapped me on the shoulder and said, "You are now a member of the choir. I will see you at choir practice 7 pm Wednesday evening." And from that moment on, my love for church music was born. In the same way, Jesus called his disciples by the lakeside, "Come, follow me." They went for many reasons, but certainly because of the force of his personality.

There was a dean of students of whom it was said that this person possessed the power to break up a student riot just by showing up. The dean didn't even have to say a word. That's the kind of presence the teacher had.

That's the kind of teacher Jesus was and is. When we meet him, the job he has in mind for us becomes a labor of love. We find comfort just by being with him. We find ourselves challenged to do things that we would never have imagined we could do. We even learn that the hard lessons of life lead also to a life of joy.

To comfort? To challenge? To learn? Yes!

CHAPTER 11

WHERE TO DRAW THE LINE

Matthew 12:30, Mark 9:38-41, Luke 9:49-50, Luke 11:23

One of the quiet joys I had during my study time in Cambridge, England was reading the journal Henri Nouwen kept during his year-long sabbatical, a year that turned out to be the final one of his life. I usually read Nouwen's journal right before I went to sleep or immediately upon arising. I often found myself resonating with what he had to say.

But nothing caught my attention more than the journal entry for Thursday, March 14, 1996. Commenting on the scripture lesson, where Jesus says, "Whoever is not with me is against me," Nouwen exclaims, "These words frighten me. I want to be with Jesus, but often it feels like I want to be with many others too!" He continues, "There is a strong tendency to play it safe. I want to stay friends with everyone. I do not like conflict or controversy. I hate division and confrontation among people." Then he asks himself, "Is this a weakness, a lack of courage to speak out forcefully, a fear of rejection, a preoccupation with being liked? Or is it a strength that allows me to bring people together and be reconciled, to create community, and to build bridges?"[1]

I remember thinking to myself, I could have said that. It's the reason I've always had trouble with this saying from Jesus. Where to draw the line is a question that has bothered me my whole ministry. I hate to draw lines that cut people off or shut them out. It's

---

1   Henri Nouwen, *Sabbatical Journey*, London: Darton, Longman and Todd Ltd 1998, p 126.

not my temperament. Yet life and ministry often demand it. Who to include on prayer chains, communion lists, nursing home and hospital visits? There is just so much time, and in some cases, just so much space in the bulletin and newsletter. There is not always room for each and everyone you might like to go see or to list. And if you do include this person, you may have to include that one next time, and so on. Precedents will be set, no matter what. So you often end up drawing lines. And I hate it.

And besides, I don't think this is what Jesus wants us to do. Yet, in this verse of scripture we hear differently. "Whoever is not with me is against me, and who does not gather with me scatters." It seems there are times when you have to draw lines. You are either in or out. As one commentary remarks about this passage, "Matthew sounds exclusive and dismissive."[1] I agree.

It helps to remember the context. The saying in Matthew comes right after the controversy with the Pharisees. They are claiming that Jesus is in league with the devil. They are not doubting that Jesus has power to heal and cast out demons. They just think he's doing it with the wrong help. They think he's acting with the aid of Satan. Jesus tries to tell them that this just doesn't make any sense. But they aren't interested in what he has to say. So it's to these people, the Pharisees, and in this particular situation, that Jesus directs his remark, "Whoever is not with me is against me." Taking the context into consideration, the hard saying begins to make some sense. Obviously, someone is not on your side if they are busy working against you.

When we turn to Mark's gospel, things seem a little more palatable and not so harsh. Mark is much more inclusive. And as you might expect, the context is different. Now it's the disciples, not the Pharisees, who are the problem. The situation seems to be this: There is a local miracle worker, someone who's not part of the group of twelve disciples. And this "outsider" is going around healing people in Jesus' name. The twelve disciples are quite concerned about this. So concerned, in fact, that they feel called upon

---

1   R.T. France, *The Gospel of Mark*, Grand Rapids: Wm. B. Eerdmans Publishing Co. 2002, p 377.

to bring the matter to Jesus' attention. They even ask Jesus if he wants them to put a stop to it.

What makes the story all the more intriguing is that it's only been a short time since the disciples themselves were out on a healing mission, and they were not as successful as this miracle worker. They were not able to drive the demons out in Jesus' name like this fellow did. How come the disciples are upset with someone who can? As they see it, the problem is that this man is not an official member of the group. He's not on Jesus' team. And to the disciples, that's worse than their not being able to work miracles. Which is worse: insiders who can't perform or an outsider who can? They obviously think it's better to be on the inside, even if you're not up to the job. How many organizations, including the church, think the same way? "Well, he may not be a very good leader, but we can trust him to do what we tell him to do."

What Jesus says to all this is revealing. His comment in Mark is warm and welcoming. It's the paradoxical opposite of what we just heard him say to the Pharisees on another occasion. Jesus tells his disciples, "Do not stop him, no one who does a work of divine power in my name will be able in the same breath to speak evil of me. For he who is not against us is on our side"(NEB). And then we learn what the real test is. "I tell you this: if anyone gives you a cup of water to drink because you are followers of the Messiah, that man assuredly will not go unrewarded" (NEB).

I think back to the early years in my ministry when we were on a rather tight budget at home. Disney World had just opened, and my wife, Susan, and I wanted to go. We saved our pennies and made sure that we stayed in a modest, but safe, hotel outside the grounds. But when we checked into our room, we found it was a beautiful suite. I went downstairs and talked with the lady at the desk. I said, "There must be some mistake. The room we have is much nicer than we can afford." She smiled and said, "I noticed on your reservation card that you are a Disciple minister. I'm a Disciple too. I thought you wouldn't mind if I upgraded you to a nicer room at no extra charge." I confess I immediately thought of these words of Jesus, "If anyone gives you a cup of water to drink because you are followers of the Messiah, that one will not go unrewarded."

A commentary I have relied on has a caption to this section of Mark's gospel that reads, "A Warning Against Cliquishness." Part of the human condition seems to be our ever vigilant concern for who's in and who's out. There's a word for it: snobbery. It's one of those *Ordinary Vices* that Judith Shklar writes about in her book by that title. Snobbery is everywhere. It's in our schools, our churches, our politics. Someone who once worked in DC told me that to understand what all the fuss is about in Washington you have to realize that it finally gets down to who's going to be invited to what parties. Will I get an invitation or not? In this regard, Jesus' words in Mark's gospel are a call to receive those we might be too eager to reject. The list is long: gays and straights, liberals and conservatives, mainline and evangelicals, Arabs and Jews, Christians and Muslims. You name it.

Jesus says that regardless of who they are, they are to be judged by the same standard. And that standard is their deeds. "By their fruits will they be known." The proof is in the pudding. If they are giving a cup of cold water to the needy, if they are making an offering to help the poor, then they are on our side. The call is to be a place of welcoming in this world where there is so much *un*welcoming.

There is a parallel in ancient history to this saying of Jesus. Cicero writes to Caesar, "We have often heard you say that while we regard everyone as enemies except those who are with us, you yourself count all those who are not against you as on your side."

Perhaps, in our day, the place where the rubber hits the road is in our relations with those outside the Christian faith, especially those of other religions. I was saddened to learn that a major religious denomination had broken ties with their world organization because they felt it was becoming too cosy with those outside the tradition. No doubt they felt they were being faithful to Jesus' words, "Those who are not with us are against us." On the other hand, I was thrilled when representatives from Jewish and Muslim faiths were included with Christians in President Reagan's funeral.

This seemed to me to be evidence in the minds of those planning the service of Jesus' other saying, "Whoever is not against me is for me." In these particular instances, Jesus' words are seemingly used to justify opposite positions and practices. Which is it? Inclusiveness or exclusiveness?

In Cambridge, England there are a lot of signs. They go up on fence posts, iron fences, grocery bulletin boards and church doors without warning at any time of the day or night. Turn around and there's another one. Some of them are about events you wouldn't want to miss. So you find yourself becoming addicted to reading signs. One of the most interesting I ran across is at King's College Chapel. There is this sign that reads, "Please do not walk on the grass." In no less than five languages! Now people from all over the world are welcome to any of King's many services free of charge. You can come and hear the magnificent choir free, just as long as you don't walk on the grass. On the one hand, it's a place of earnest welcome. Standing in line, you're likely to hear any number of languages being spoken, Dutch, French, English, Japanese, German. On the other hand, the rules are frankly and abruptly restrictive. You are not to walk on the grass, and if you do, you will find that someone appears out of nowhere to set you straight. Perhaps the way they go about it at King's is a hint as to how we might begin to put together these two sayings of Jesus which on the surface seems so contradictory.

Anyone who compares the gospel accounts in Matthew, Mark and Luke of these particular sayings of Jesus, cannot help but notice that Mark has the inclusive one, Matthew, the exclusive one, and Luke has them both. Maybe, by including both sayings, Luke is saying that the truth is in the tension between the two.

Several suggestions have been raised as to why Luke retained both sayings. The most helpful one to me is the suggestion that the exclusive saying is to be used when we are examining ourselves, and the inclusive one is in our dealings with others. Sadly, sometimes we get the two confused and apply them in just the opposite way Jesus intended.

Let me attempt to show you what I mean. "Whoever is not for me is against me." This is to be used when we are trying to size up our personal relationship with Jesus. It's meant to be the standard by which we judge our own commitment and loyalty to Christ. It's a way of determining how faithful we are in our commitment. Are we with him or not? Finally, there is only one way to answer that question.

But when it comes to determining who our allies are, we are to use the broader, more tolerant saying. "Whoever is not against us is for us." We join hands in the work that needs to be done for God with all who would like to help out. It's been summed up this way: "Ecumenical openness and unambiguous demand for a clear confession of Jesus are certainly compatible."[1] In this world of ours, there will always be insiders and outsiders, opponents and friends, make no mistake of it. When it comes to dealing with ourselves, we are not to let ourselves off the hook. We are to use the harder saying in examining our conscience. But when it comes to dealing with those outside, we are to use a more tolerant and inclusive approach. Most of all, when dealing with others, we are to be extremely cautious about where we draw the line. Otherwise we might find ourselves excluding some people Jesus would prefer to include.

In this world we are called upon to draw lines, and always will be. But before we do, let us be absolutely certain whether the line is to keep us in or others out.

To get back to those signs in Cambridge, most, if not all, of the thirty-three colleges that make up the University have brick walls and gates which define them. The balcony of our flat in Wesley House overlooked the brick walled court of Sussex College. And as we were on the "Hop-on-Hop-Off" tour route of Cambridge, we became accustomed to hearing the tour guide, usually an elderly lady, remark in her intriguing accent several times a day as they passed our way, "Next on your left is Jesus College, with one of the most beautiful gates in Cambridge." I'm not sure if all these walls

1   W.D. Davies and Dale C. Allison, *Matthew Vol 2*, Edinburgh: T&T Clark 1991, p 344.

and gates are meant to keep the students in or the townspeople out. Maybe a little of both. What I do know, though, is this: as you are walking around this quaint medieval city, every so often, you come upon a small sandwich board sign placed along the walkway of the gate to the college. The sign board often says something like, "Organ Concert at 6:00 pm; Evensong at 6:30 pm; All are welcome." In some similar fashion, unintrusive, but welcoming, is a way the church of Jesus Christ can reach out to the world in the days to come.

CHAPTER 12

THE LIMITS OF FORGIVENESS

Matthew 18:15-35

There always seems to be somebody who likes to break the rules. Or if not break them, at least try to find a way to get around them.

This begins as soon as we learn to talk. There are an amazing number of ways that a small child can dodge going to bed. "Read me another story, Daddy. May I have juice? I need my dinosaur before I can go to sleep. I just want to watch the video one more time." Or, if none of these work, there's the last resort of outright rebellion, the temper tantrum.

Come the teen years, the stakes are even higher when curfew is seen as repressive of the youth's desire for freedom. The dodge can take the form of lying, or have someone else do it for you. "Yes, George was over at my house last night." There are as many, if not more, creative ways to get around the rules at this age as there was when the child was younger. And every teacher in the classroom knows that high school men and women can find a loophole where there is none to be found. "But you did not say that we had to have the paper in by class time today. I was planning on working on it later today during study hall and then give it to you before the end of school."

Our church life, especially the committee life of a congregation, is not free of this struggle either. Hand out a sheet of paper with the minutes of the meeting and invariably someone will ask, "Did we decide to do that the last time we were here? I certain-

ly don't remember that." It's one of the most beloved games that
church people like to play to get around the rules.

What results from all of these situations is tension, if not conflict. And then the togetherness of the community is in jeopardy.
How can I stay in this group that's bent on making my life misera-
ble? How can I continue to associate with those who obviously do
not appreciate what I have to say? These kinds of questions bring
to mind Winston Churchill's definition of democracy. "Democracy
is the occasional necessity of deferring your own opinion to that of
someone else." That's one way to avoid disruption and to keep the
group together, and on task.

There's another sly way that congregations have of derailing
the mission. A simple question can cause the train to jump the
track. At some point in the meeting, a supposedly well-meaning
committee member says, "I'm bringing this up because I know no
one else will." At which the leader of the committee can be heard
mumbling under their breath, "Yes, no one would bring it up unless
you did." And so conflict begins, as so often it does, with a question,
"Has anyone thought about what would happen if we did this?"

And what about those times when things get out of hand
to the point where a member openly threatens to pull out of the
process or actually goes through with it? "Well, if this is what this
church stands for, I can no longer be a part of it." How do you stay
together at times like these?

Two ways come to mind. One is to try to find a way so that
the offended member can save face. Or if that's not possible, another way is to come to the point where forgiveness is offered and
accepted by the offending parties. Finding a way to avoid a rupture
is often difficult. A sensitive leader might remark, "Now I know we
all want to find a way to do this together, don't we? As a member
of this search committee, I personally want everyone to go along
with whatever we finally agree on."

Take the account in Matthew's gospel about reproving a brother or sister who sins against the fellowship. It seems to have been
drawn up by the early church on the basis of what they believed
to be Jesus' intention for his followers. Or as others believe, the

account may go back to Jesus, himself. Either way, Matthew 18:15-35 is a place to begin in considering how we might handle these messy situations that are encountered in family or church. Taken together, these verses in Matthew's gospel contain a secret of how to stay together, as well as the limits of forgiveness.

Interestingly, the focus is not so much on what the *offender* should do as on the way the *offended* are to behave. "If another member of the church sins against you, go and point out the fault when the two of you are alone." First, try to contain the harm in as tight a circle as possible. Many of us have been in the painful experience of having to decide what to do when a friend is thinking of divorce. It's even more complicated when we are friends of both parties. Whom do you go to see first, or should you even go to see either party? From personal experience, I've learned that the worst thing is to do nothing. Invariably, that way we are certain to lose at least one, if not two friends. Following the Biblical way of personal confrontation provides a way to start. It's a tried and true means of reconciling and maintaining a friendship. I've had friends contemplating divorce tell me that regardless of how it all turned out, they were glad that I came to talk directly to them and did not speak about them behind their backs.

Of course, there is always the matter of readiness on the part of those who need to hear. They may or may not be ready to listen. As in most cases, timing is everything. Putting it off usually just means neglect. The point of the exercise is in these words, "If the member listens to you, you have regained that one." Whatever we do, we should never lose sight that staying in relationship is the ultimate goal.[1]

But what if that doesn't work? That's the next situation Matthew takes up. The next best advice is to broaden the circle, just a little. Seek out two or three trusted individuals to help if you are not successful in the one-on-one confrontation. "Take one or two others along with you, so that every word may be confirmed by the evidence of the two or three witnesses." Right off, whatever was

---

1   Daniel Patte, *The Gospel According to Matthew*, Philadelphia, Pennsylvania: Fortress Press 1987, p 253-258.

the cause for the discontent in the fellowship; it could not have been a little matter, if what's being said needs the confirmation of witnesses. It's hoped that the added presence of a couple of concerned members might just bring about repentance on the part of the offender. But then again, it might not. It might just add fuel to the fire. It's impossible to know in advance.

So the strategy is to widen the circle of accountability even more. "If the member refuses to listen to them, tell it to the church; and if the offender refuses to listen even to the church, let such a one be to you as a Gentile and a tax collector." In light of Jesus' association with these two kinds of people in his ministry on earth, there are some who think that these words tell us more about the state of the church at the time the words were written than it does about Jesus himself. Regardless, the use of harsh words does indicate the extent to which the situation has descended. Things have deteriorated to the point that all involved are now desperate. This advice in Jesus' words is a defacto way of stating the situation. By now, those who have committed the dastardly deed, whatever it was, have chosen to become outcasts. By this time, there is nothing more the community can do about it. Sadly, these kinds of occurrences happen from time to time, even in our best efforts at reconciliation. At this point, it may seem that the end result of all our attempts at reconciliation has reached the limit of forgiveness.

I've noticed this about the teachings of Jesus. Search long enough and hard enough, and you can almost always find a saying or two which balances whatever teaching that may be giving you a hard time. For instance, this "hard" saying in Matthew 18:17 about beloved friends becoming outcasts, like Gentiles and tax collectors, is closely followed in verses 21-22 with Jesus' "soft" teachings on forgiveness. "Then Peter came and said to him, "Lord, if another member of the church sins against me, how often should I forgive? As many as seven times?" Some historical background is helpful in giving Peter his due. Surely, Peter must have known that the rabbis had determined that three times was the extent to which an individual was required to go in offering forgiveness. And evidently, Peter had been around Jesus long enough to realize that the rabbis' determination of three times was not gracious enough in the eyes of Jesus. So Peter has doubled that amount and more to "Seven times?" Jesus replies, "Not seven times, but, I tell you, seventy times seven." Now it doesn't take a rocket scientist to realize that Jesus is not speaking literally. It's not a matter of counting, but of being and staying in relationship. And, lest we miss the point about forgiveness, or get hung up on calculating how much is seventy times seven– that is, how many times should we forgive– Jesus tells a story to demonstrate how it all works out in practice.

The story is the parable of the Unforgiving Servant. This is one of the clearest parables to see a main point of Jesus' teachings. It's one of many Parables of the Kingdom. The king in the parable is remarkably like the Heavenly Father Jesus reveals by his words and deeds, as he moves about the cities and towns of Galilee.

There comes a time when this king wishes to settle accounts. In the words of a famous theologian, "There is a deadline on our lives. Every day is judgment day." So when the king begins to make good on settling his accounts, a slave who owed him 10,000 talents was brought before him. (A talent is the largest measure in the mid-East, and to say that a man owed 10,000 talents would be like saying that he was in debt more than a million dollars.) There was no way the slave could ever repay the king no matter how long he worked. So the king ordered the man, along with his wife and children, together with all his possessions, to be sold as payment for the debt. What the king ordered was standard practice in that day.

But the slave, evidently displaying a prior knowledge and relationship with the king, falls on his knees and begs the king, "Have patience with me, and I will pay you everything." But the king is not to be taken in by the man's plea. The king knows that there's no way the man can even make a dent in the amount of debt, no matter how long he worked to pay it off. But "out of pity" the Lord of that slave released him and forgave him. The king was not only a wise king, but a good man who acted out of compassion.

Now we might expect the story to end with this man rejoicing and giving thanks to his Master for what had been done for him. But not so. This same slave, no sooner than he has left the presence of the good king, comes upon one of his fellow slaves who owes him money, actually a much smaller amount. The forgiven slave seizes his comrade by the throat and says, "Pay what you owe." Whether or not this fellow had witnessed what had transpired earlier between the indebted slave and the king, this fellow slave follows suit, falls down and pleads with the forgiven slave to forgive him. But to no avail. In an act of retaliation, the previously forgiven slave has the slave who owed him thrown into prison. And it just so happened, that there were those standing by who had seen what had taken place. They were greatly disturbed by what they had seen, and so they went and told the king about it.

Then the king again summoned the slave who had been forgiven and said to him, "You wicked slave! I forgave you all that debt because you pleaded with me. Should you not have had mercy on your fellow slave, as I had mercy on you?" In the words of today's world, "Could you not have paid it forward?" "And in anger his lord handed him over to be tortured until he would pay his entire debt," which, as we now understand, meant that the slave would be in jail forever.

Jesus concludes the story with these words. "So my heavenly Father will also do to every one of you, if you do not forgive your brother or sister from your heart." Failing to forgive our brothers and sisters is tantamount to failing to be like God. The Fifth Beatitude, "Blessed are the merciful, for they shall obtain mercy," is turned upside down.

As we move along the parable, according to Jesus, forgiveness should have no limits. Yet, not everyone will accept that. While the king values the relationship he has with his slave more than what the slave owes him, the slave does not. Not everyone always gets the point. The bottom line is that those who will not forgive cannot expect to be forgiven. As the Lord's Prayer so clearly states it, God's willingness to forgive us depends on our willingness to forgive others. "Forgive us our sins, as we forgive those who have sinned against us."

Yet, as with all the teachings of Jesus, there is no guarantee that everything will turn out all right. There is instead the promise of a reward. Following Jesus' way is simply not as easy as many of us wish it to be. Even when we do muster up the gumption to forgive someone who has hurt us, like the slave in the parable, they may not in turn forgive us.

Once as their senior pastor, the church I served had to let a member of the staff go. When we did, a member in the congregation became furious with me for allowing this to take place. It was not long before I began receiving reports that this individual was going around town saying things about me that were untrue. It hurt deeply. First, because it was untrue, and secondly because I couldn't believe anyone in the church could act like that. I resolved to make amends. I took the first step outlined by Matthew. I confronted the person privately. I told them that I wanted to heal the broken relationship we shared. Without so much as a thought, the person looked at me and said, "You may, but I don't." I was left high and dry, holding the bag. By then, I was so hurt that I could not bring myself to do more.

Looking back on this incident from years ago, I wonder what would have happened had I pursued the other two options outlined by Matthew? The only thing I can say for sure is that to this day I know in my heart that I did the right thing to offer forgiveness. And maybe that's what Jesus is trying to say all along. The offer of forgiveness, even when refused, is reward enough. To this day, while I regret the incident ever happened, I have a clear conscience. And while that's a beginning to the secret of staying together, many times it is also a lesson in the limits of forgiveness. The limit of forgiveness is when it is refused.[1] And even God, says Jesus, is not able to forgive someone who cannot receive it.

---

1   Daniel J. Harrington, *The Gospel According to Matthew*, Collegeville, Minnesota: The Liturgical Press 1983, p 79.

CHAPTER 13

TURN THE OTHER CHEEK?

Luke 6:27-36, Luke 12:49-53, Luke 19:41-48, Luke 22:35-38, 47-53, Luke 23:34

Surely, one of our goals as Christians is to live at peace with ourselves and with one another. Yet, that's not always as simple as it might appear. In fact, this honorable goal is often observed more in its breach than in achievement. Good Christians are often found on both sides of peace and justice issues. But from a Christian standpoint, is violence, personal or otherwise, only justified in self-defense, or can a case be made that there are times when it is a necessary evil, especially if the evil you are fighting is big enough? In the words of Jesus, should we turn the cheek? Or is there a time when that simple command is not to be followed?

Evidently that's what Larry Huch, a Texas pastor and a regional director of Christians United for Israel, thinks. He uses Jesus' own words against him. Defending Israel's right to self-defense in the conflict in Lebanon, Huch says outright, "We will not turn the other cheek."[1] Personally, I think it's one thing to say something like this and another not to acknowledge that we are deeply sorry that we do not feel that at the moment we can put Jesus' teachings into practice.

Yet, even on the childhood playground it's not always easy to know what to do. My first, personal lesson in the appropriateness or inappropriateness of striking back came when my neighborhood friend, Anna Dean, hit me in the stomach while we were kids

---

1 *National Catholic Reporter*, July 28 as quoted in *The Christian Century*, Aug 22, 2006, p 7.

laying under the big elm tree in my front yard. In an instant, I hit her back. The moment I did, I thought to myself, "Boy, am I in for trouble." Of course, I never told my parents what I had done, and I hoped that she wouldn't tell hers. But that's exactly what she did. The next day my mother asked me straight out, "Did you hit Anna Dean?" I knew better than to lie about it. By this time, I'd been to too many Sunday School classes and listened to too many sermons to try to fake it. So, I replied, "Yes, I did." To my credit, I must have thought that owning up to my misdeed was the right thing to do. "David," I heard my mother say, "Why did you do it?" "Because she hit me first." As if that justified everything. And while I was expecting to be reprimanded heartily for what I had done, I couldn't believe my ears at what came next. "Well," said my mother, "I don't want you ever to do that again. But for what it's worth, Anna Dean's parents told me not to get on you for hitting back." They told her, "If David Cartwright hit you, then you must have had it coming." I was both elated and confused. Elated to have gotten off the hook so easily and confused as to why I was not punished. Didn't I deserve to be punished for what I had done? Wasn't what I did wrong? Did not Jesus say, "If anyone strikes you on the cheek, offer the other also?" But in my case, I was almost applauded for my actions.

To this day, I remain confused, as I dare say most people are, not to mention those of us who call ourselves Christians. Are we not confused about whether violence in any form is appropriate? Surely, it could not be plainer than when Jesus says, "Love your enemies, do good to those who hate you, bless those who curse you, pray for those who abuse you."

And yet, as any child knows, we live in a world of conflicting messages when it comes to practicing these teachings of Jesus. We teach our children not to pick a fight, but at the same time, we also teach them that if someone picks a fight with them, they are to win. If not, what's that punch line about? "You should have seen the other guy." Isn't that the American way?

It doesn't matter whether it's war or capital punishment, domestic violence in the home, corporal discipline at school, crime in the streets or rage on the roads, it's harder and harder for some of us to square our actions with these simple teachings of Jesus. Or is part of the problem that these teachings are not as simple as they seem?

Sometimes discord just happens. It may even be the natural result of a perfectly good action or idea. What else could provoke Jesus to say at one point in his ministry, "I came to bring fire to the earth, and how I wish it were already kindled! I have a baptism with which to be baptized, and what stress I am under until it is completed! Do you think that I have come to bring peace to the earth? No, I tell you, but rather division!" Other gospel writers are more explicit: "Not peace, but a sword." Then Jesus goes on to outline how his mission announcing the coming of the Kingdom of God will at times result in families being cut in two, father against son, son against father, mother against daughter, and so on. Loyalty to Jesus' cause may at times result in conflict with other loyalties we already have, such as family and work. And that's exactly what happened to many families back then. Following Christ tore families apart rather than bringing them together.

It can still happen. I've seen it in families when someone's faith forbids them to attend the funeral of a family member. Nothing intentional, mind you; nothing personal, that's just the way it is. But discord and possible lasting hurt are sown nonetheless. Yes, sometimes even when we're trying to be good, it can turn out the other way. Some violence, or should I say disruption, is due to the natural outcome of otherwise good intentions. At least that's the way I understand what Jesus meant by bringing a sword. Unfortunately, the sword is double-edged. It cuts two ways.

But is violence ever justified? Some of Jesus' teachings suggest that it never is; yet his actions can be viewed otherwise.

A case in point. What are we to make of Jesus' disturbance in the temple? As I read Luke, the cleansing of the temple appears to take place late on Palm Sunday. Earlier in the day, Jesus is looking down on the city of Jerusalem from the Mount of Olives. As he weeps over the city, Jesus utters words that pierce our hearts to this day: "If you, even you, had only recognized on this day the things that make for peace!" The point is, of course, that if they could have seen Jesus as the Bringer of Peace, they would not be in for as much heartache and bloodshed in the days to come.

The tears on Jesus' face quickly turn into words of anger from his mouth and wild actions with his hands as he enters the temple and begins to drive out the money changers. "It is written, 'My house shall be a house of prayer;' but you have made it a den of robbers." Other gospels fill us in about the use of a whip and the overturning of the tables. Luke, while softening the blow, still manages to capture the hearts and imaginations of Christians down the ages. And at times this event in the temple has been used to justify specific acts of violence. But is this a proper use of the scripture? If we mean by that, is it ever right to get mad, especially when something sacred is being abused or misused, I would say yes. But remember, no one was killed that day in the temple. And to those who think that Jesus' action gives them the right to lash out at everything they feel is against the will of God, I would urge a great deal of caution.

Jesus' actions in the temple imply to me that there are occasions that can justify taking matters into our own hands. Sometimes it's necessary to clean house. But we'd better be awfully sure that we know what we're doing. Maybe this is why even Jesus' own disciples were at times confused about their Master's teachings on violence.

Four days later, on the day that would later be called, Maundy Thursday, Jesus is still trying to teach his disciples a thing or two. It's like a last minute cramming session or pulling an all-nighter. Among so many other teachings, there is this enigmatic passage: "When I sent you out without a purse, bag or sandals, did you lack anything?" They said, "No, not a thing." He said to them, "But now, the one who has a purse must take it, and likewise a bag. And the one who has no sword must sell his cloak and buy a new one."

What? Did I hear Jesus correctly? Sell the outer garment that protects you from the elements to purchase a sword, more likely, the ever-present Mid-Eastern dagger? Give up a garment that could also be used as a sleeping bag to buy a weapon? Times have certainly changed from when Jesus told them to go out like beggar monks with nothing to protect or defend themselves! Has Jesus changed his mind or lost it? Or do new events justify the change? Do "new occasions teach new duties," as the hymn says? What's behind all this?

To fulfill scripture, that's part of it. "'And he was content among the lawless;' and indeed what is written about me is being fulfilled."

But there is more. "They (the disciples) said, "Lord, look, here are two swords." He replied, "It is enough." Two things catch my attention. First, evidently, some of the disciples are carrying swords. I almost said that they were *still* carrying swords. But that assumes that they might have been asked to give them up, but did not. I don't know about that. All I know is, at this late stage in the game, the swords are there.

Secondly, what does Jesus mean when he says, "It is enough." Does he mean that two weapons are sufficient? Or does he mean that the weapons being present are symbolic of what is shortly to take place? Or does he mean that the die is cast? Events have been set into motion. There's no turning back. If I had to choose, I would say something like that. But the real lesson is that there are times when we present-day disciples are just as confused as the first ones were that night when Jesus was betrayed.

However, according to Luke's gospel, things continue to get even more puzzling. As the darkness deepens, Jesus is praying on the Mount of Olives while his disciples sleep. As the temple police approach with Judas, who will betray Jesus with that famous kiss, some of the disciples say to Jesus, "Lord, should we strike with the sword?" Even at this late hour, the question itself is an indication that the disciples are utterly and hopelessly confused about the use of force under these dire circumstances. Not waiting for an answer from Jesus, one disciple – John's gospel tells us it was Peter – strikes the servant of the high priest, cutting off the servant's ear. This time Luke tells us that Jesus is quick to respond, "No more of this." And what's more, Jesus touches the servant's ear and heals him. Compassionate, even under the most severe pressure, Jesus does the merciful act of taking care of an innocent bystander. He heals the servant's ear.

I became addicted to BBC TV programs while I was on sabbatical in England with my wife, Susan. So much so that when we came back to the States we subscribed to digital cable TV so that we could get BBC America. Now we are feeding our addiction here at home. Our latest fixation is *Sharpe's Adventures* set in Spain during the Napoleonic wars. It's an epic about a street ruffian who rose through the ranks to become a larger-than-life British military officer by the name of Sharpe. In one episode, Sharpe is captured in India while trying to rescue a friend. The plot is rather complicated, but there is a scene involving two French officers who have deserted from serving their country and have gone over to the Indian side. The two Frenchmen are standing by watching the cruel and unusual punishment of English prisoners of war ordered by a deserted English officer who has also defected to the Indian side. (I said the plot was complicated.) One of these Frenchmen whispers to the other, "I thought there were rules even in war." The other officer shrugs his shoulders, as if to say, "We can do nothing." Later, this French officer comes to his senses and joins Sharpe in defeating the renegade Indians. Sharpe asks him the reason for his turnabout. The Frenchman answers, "There have to be rules, even in war."

When Jesus healed the servant's ear, he was saying much the same thing that night even as he was under arrest. It's not right for the innocent to get hurt in a conflict that has nothing to do with them.

Finally, the forces of evil have their day, and Jesus is crucified like a common criminal amid common criminals. In Luke's gospel, the very first thing, mind you, that Jesus says as he hangs on the cross, are some of the most memorable words in the history of the world. "Father, forgive them, for they do not know what they are doing." Early in his ministry, Jesus had taught that we are to love our enemies. Now on the cross, he's doing just that.

As a part of my ministry near a university campus, I enjoyed guiding student interns almost every summer. For several years, as a basis for our study sessions, we used an excellent book, *Practicing Our Faith*. In the chapter on forgiveness, there's a story that shows how one family was able to follow in Jesus' footsteps.

"A twelve-year-old boy named John was playing one day with the nine-year old-girl who lived next door. Her name was Marie. Unfortunately, they found a loaded pistol in a drawer and before long their make-believe game turned into a tragic nightmare and little Marie was dead. Everyone in the small town attended the funeral of the little girl, everyone except John, who could not face anyone and refused to talk with anyone.

"The morning after the funeral, Marie's older brother went next door to talk with John. "John, come with me," he said. "I want to take you to school." John refused, saying, "I never want to see anyone again. I wish it was me who was dead." The brother insisted and finally persuaded John to go with him. The brother talked with the school principal and asked him to call a special assembly. Five hundred and eighty students filed into the gymnasium. Marie's brother stood before them and said, "A terrible thing has happened; my little sister was accidentally shot by one of your fellow class-mates. This is one of those tragedies that mars life. Now I want you all to know that my family and John's family have been to church together this morning and we shared in Holy Communion." Then he called John next to him, put his arm around his shoulders, and continued, "This boy's future depends much on us. My family has forgiven John because we love him. Marie would want that. And I ask you to love and forgive him, too. Then he hugged John, and they wept together."[1]

It's a lesson Nelson Mandela had to learn as well. He said that the day he left prison, he realized that if he continued to hate those who had held him hostage there for so many years, he would still be in prison even though he was out.

To turn the cheek? Well, yes. No. Maybe. Perhaps it depends on circumstances. The scriptural record is ambiguous.

But this much I do know: Let us always try to do good and be at peace with ourselves and others, regardless of circumstances. Let that be our goal. But realize that discord and violence are bound to occur at times. Even good things can result in a bad outcome

---

1   Dorothy C. Bass, editor; *Practicing Our Faith*, San Francisco: Josey Bass Publishers 1997 p 141-142.

for some. Jesus' message of good news was not good for everyone. There may be times when due to the level of misuse and abuse, we may even be called to take matters into our own hands. But at these times, let us always make sure that we are on target, like Jesus was that day in the temple. Violence, however a necessary evil, is never for violence's sake. At the very least, let us never lose sight of the innocent. Like Jesus, we are to have concern for the servant's ear. Ultimately, violence should be redemptive, like Jesus forgiving his enemies on the cross, Marie's older brother taking little John to school, or Nelson Mandela forgiving his oppressors. The goal is to transform a hostile situation into a peaceful one.

These simple teachings of Jesus have a way of becoming very complex when we try to put them into practice. They take the best thinking and praying we can muster. But with that said, Jesus' way is still the best way I know to live in a hostile world and not lash out.

CHAPTER 14

WHAT A WAY TO DIE!

Mark 15:31-38, Luke 23:26-46

I was once asked to see a woman who was dying. She was not a member of the church I was serving at the time, but many people in the congregation knew her. She had lots of friends. She was known for being a light-hearted, fun loving person. Anyone would like to call her their friend. But at the time I was asked to visit her, she had become very bitter. She felt God had let her down. She was sick and dying from cancer. She doted on her only son, something that as an only child I could identify with. Her son was a very successful young man who had just graduated from college, and was planning on getting married the coming fall to his lovely fiancé.

The problem was the doctors had told this woman that most likely she would not be around for the wedding. So she was fighting mad with God. As far as she was concerned, God had simply let her down. Her cancer couldn't have come at a worse time. By the time I was called in to see what I could do, she was in alternating bouts of anger and depression.

The first time that I visited her she was in bed, surrounded by many beautiful things. It was about the most beautiful bedroom I had seen. It looked like it came right out of *House Beautiful* or *Architectural Digest*. (I immediately thought of that phrase from Harry Emerson Fosdick's great hymn, "rich in things and poor in soul.")

When I entered the room, she had her back to the door. I introduced myself. Not bothering to turn over, she grunted, "I guess they've sent for you to get me to forgive God."

I said, "Well, that's not exactly what I was asked to do. I was only asked if I would come and see you. I can come back another time, if it would be more convenient."

At this, she turned over and looked me up one side and down the other.

I said, "Is there anything I can do for you?"

"No, I'm beyond help."

"Would you like a prayer?" I asked.

She replied, "No, thank you."

"Would you like for me to come back?"

"That's up to you," she said.

And that was the end of our visit.

The next few visits didn't go much better. Over the next months, I visited her several times, and she gradually began to warm up. Finally, she opened up and shared her disappointment about not being able to see her son's wedding, which as it turned out, the doctors were right, and she didn't. We even talked about how mad she was with God. I told her God could take it. Even Jesus got mad at God that day on the cross. "My God, my God, why have you forsaken me!" he screamed. But I went on to say, "He didn't stop there. It didn't end that way." Finally, I said, "If you know you're going to die, and everyone agrees that's what's going to happen, is this the way you want to go? Is this the legacy you want to leave your son? Is this the last memory you want him to have of you? All of this pain and disappointment? You know, what you're doing is not a very good way to die, if you ask me." At first, she was startled at my abruptness. But by this time, we had established a relationship that could take it. She looked at me and said, "I guess you're right. I'd better make some changes; and – in a hurry." We prayed for repentance, for forgiveness, and for the power to surrender, three things that Luke lifts up for us as Jesus is dying on the cross. I'm glad to be able to tell you that after all this pain and struggle, she died peacefully.

When the movie, *The Passion of the Christ*, came out, there was a lot of talk about how much suffering Jesus went through on our behalf. And I don't want to diminish that one whit, not in the least. But what has always struck me about the crucifixion is not the amount of suffering Jesus went through, but how he handled it. We Christians used to talk about "dying the good death." Some of our hymns sing about it.

James Montgomery's words reverently capture the idea:

Go to dark Gethsemane.
Cal'vry's mountain climb.
There adoring at his feet, mark the miracle of time,
God's own sacrifice complete;
'It is finished!' hear the cry;
learn of Jesus Christ how to die."

The last thing we have to do on this earth is to die. And how we do it, I think, will say a lot about the lives we've been living.

Currently, there's also a lot of talk about dying with dignity. The hospice program is dedicated to that. I'm continually impressed with how comforting their services are to those who need them. But there is Someone we can look to, beyond the resources this earth can provide. And that is to Jesus, the Christ, as we see him on the cross. How Jesus handled his death is a model for the way we can handle ours.

And a way to do this is to look at the words from the cross Luke has preserved for us. There are "Last Words" of Jesus in the other gospels, but Luke's passion story above all others, shows us a picture of One who knew how to die a noble death. As I read Luke's account of the Passion, it's almost as if Luke is looking at the crucifixion and thinking, "My, what a way to die!" In a world where death is still, as the Apostle Paul put it, "the last enemy to be destroyed," finding a way to die is no little thing.

Jesus did not die alone that first Good Friday. In fact, according to the gospels, he was one of three crucified that day. Hanging alongside him was a criminal who taunted: "Some Messiah you are! Save yourself! Save us!"

But the other one made him shut up: "Have you no fear of God? You're getting the same as him. We deserve this, but not him– he did nothing to deserve this." Then he said, "Jesus, remember me when you enter your kingdom."

He said, "Don't worry, I will. Today you will join me in paradise."[1]

This thief– the good thief we call him–is repentant. He's turning his life around. Albeit at the last minute, but better late than never. And Jesus recognizes his repentance for what it is. The man is sorry for his sins. And he wants to be where Jesus is, wherever that may be. So Jesus says to him the words we all hope to hear, "Today, you will join me in paradise."

The literal meaning of the word "paradise" is a garden or a park. In oriental society to this day, important, intimate events take place in gardens. You don't just take anyone for a stroll in the park. Think of all the important announcements that have been issued in the Rose Garden of the White House; all of the many treaties that have been signed there, Arafat and Rabin shaking hands in 1993 is one of the biggest. When Jesus says to the good thief, "Today, you will join me in paradise," he's telling him, "Where I am, you will be also."

The way from here to there is repentance. We have to leave aside a lot of baggage to go for a walk with God in his garden. It's hard to walk with suitcases in your hands. The first step is to repent. It's one thing we can only do for ourselves. We mean it when we say we're sorry for the things we've messed up in life. It's one of the most important things we can do in this life. It's also one of the most necessary things we do when we come to face death. Like the thief on the cross, we need to repent. And when we do, we hear God's gracious promise, "Today, you will join me in paradise!" What a way to die!

A little earlier, hanging there on the cross, Jesus does something that, I personally think, is extraordinary beyond most anything we see on this earth. As he's being crucified, Jesus exclaims, "Father, forgive them; they don't know what they're doing." Of course, they didn't! How could they? But they thought they did, and that only made matters worse. How much harm has been done by well-meaning people who thought they knew what they were doing and did not!

1   Eugene H Peterson, *The Message*, Colorado Springs: Navpress 1993, p 181.

Dying on the cross, Jesus forgives them, all of them. The Romans, the Jews, the High Priest, the Disciples, Judas – the bad thief, all who've had a hand in it, including us, when "we have done the things that we should not have done and not done the things that we should have done."

But Jesus shows us the way out. If repentance is the key that opens the door, forgiveness is the door itself. There's no better way to live in this world, than to forgive those who've harmed us. When it comes to leaving this world, it's absolutely necessary if we are to die in peace.

Perhaps you know about the Women in Black. They are an international organization. They began as mainly Israeli women who wear the garb of Palestinian women, and gather each Sabbath at the Wailing Wall in Jerusalem. They're devoted to promoting peace between Jews and Arabs in Israel. They say a prayer, a Kaddish, the Jewish prayer for the dead. They first pray for all the Israelis who have died that week. Then they pray for all the Palestinians who have died. While they are saying their prayers, they routinely have to endure insults, curses, spitting. Sometimes they're even stoned. This has been going on every week for years.

Not too long ago, an Israeli mother's daughter was killed by a suicide bomber. This is what the mother had to say, "For me, the enemy is not the Palestinian people. For me, the struggle is not between Palestinians and Israelis, nor between Jews and Arabs. There are only two kinds of people in the world: those who seek peace and those who seek war. My people are those who seek peace."[1]

Sounds a lot like Jesus dying on the cross, doesn't it? "Father, forgive them. For they do not know what they're doing." As a model for living, it can't be beat; as a picture of how to die, it cannot be surpassed. To reach out in forgiveness to our enemies, what a way to die!

Eugene Peterson tells it this way: "By now it was noon. The whole earth became dark, the darkness lasting three hours – a total blackout. The Temple curtain split right down the middle. Jesus

---

1   Megan McKenna, *The New Stations of the Cross*, USA: Doubleday 2003, p 76-77.

called loudly, "Father, I place my life in your hands." Then he breathed his last.[1]

For my part, in these last words of Jesus, Luke has given us a perfect example of how to die, of how to bring our lives to a close.

Many of the words that Jesus says on the cross actually come from the Psalms. As he's dying, Jesus reaches down inside himself, and brings to mind scriptures that he had been taught as a child. This last phrase, "Father, into your hands I commit my spirit," is from Psalm 31, verse 5. This is a prayer Jewish mothers teach their children when they put them to bed at night. It's like, "Now, I lay me down to sleep, I pray the Lord, my soul to keep. If I should die before I wake, I pray the Lord, my soul to take."

Luke is telling us that in spite of all the agony and suffering Jesus went through, Jesus kept his childhood trust in God. And as he dies, he shows us how to.

And something else. Throughout his ministry, Jesus had taught that unless we become as little children, we can never hope to enter the kingdom of heaven. Now, hanging on the cross, Jesus is practicing what he preached, even under the most severe torture. Like a child saying his bedtime prayers, hanging there dying on the cross, Jesus falls to sleep, safe in his Father's arms, with a childhood prayer on his lips, completely surrendering his life to God. What a way to die!

Once when a good friend of mine was dying from cancer, I said to him, "Are we talking about what you need to talk about?" Through the pain and the drugs, he looked at me and said, "David, sometimes it just comes down to you and God."

And so it does.

---

1   Eugene H Peterson, *The Message*, Colorado Springs: Navpress 1993, p 181-182.

CHAPTER 15

WE WILL RISE!

John 11:17-27, John 12:20-26

As a pastor, each Lent, I loved leading the youth inquirers' classes on church membership. I especially cherished it when it resulted in the confessing of their faith and being baptized, as happened many times over during the course of my ministry. But there's another reason I loved to work with this age. You never quite knew what these fifth and sixth graders were going to come up with. Once, when we were talking about the resurrection, I asked if anyone in the class knew what it was. One member eagerly put her hand up and said, "I know. It's when Jesus got up from the dead and walked out of the tomb and went straight to heaven. Now that's something you don't see every day!" I couldn't keep from laughing. It was so refreshingly true! From the mouths of babes!

No, you don't see that every day, but the fact is, you only have to see it once for it to be true. It only has to happen once to make all the difference in the world! We call the day it took place Easter. And that's why so many of us show up in church each Easter. We all want to hear again the story about how it happened. We want to know what it means for us today and forever.

One of my favorite movies is *The Lion in Winter*. There's one memorable line where sharp-tongued Eleanor of Aquitaine (Kathryn Hepburn) says to King Henry (Peter O'Toole): "In a world where carpenters are resurrected, anything is possible!" That in a nutshell is the truth of Easter. Anything is possible with God, even someone coming back from the dead. One miracle is all we need to prove it. One instance is enough. That's why the Apostle Paul calls Jesus "the first fruits of those who have fallen asleep." Jesus is simply the first of many to come.

Actually, there are hints along the way. Especially, at the time of the year when Spring returns waking everything up from a long winter sleep. There are many analogies in this world that beautifully display nature's process of death and renewal. Jesus himself once told a parable using natural elements that he saw everywhere around him. Interestingly, this parable comes to us only in the gospel of John. None of the other gospels have it.

"Very truly, I tell you, unless a grain of wheat falls into the earth and dies, it remains just a single grain; but if it dies, it bears much fruit."

How naturally true that is. It rings true to our ears the moment we hear it. Of course, Jesus is referring, first of all, to his own death, and then to ours, when he teaches this lesson. The point is easy to grasp, even though it sounds strangely paradoxical. Death while appearing to be the opposite of life is actually the means to gain life. Just as Jesus' death on the cross appeared to be the end, in truth, it was the means to bring *life* to all. That's why we call it *Good* Friday. And that's why the Church of Sweden suggests that a sheaf of wheat be placed on the casket at funerals, instead of the customary flowers we American Christians are used to.

Father Raymond Brown wisely points out that the contrast is between dying and bearing fruit, not about dying and remaining unproductive.[1] We might have expected that Jesus would go on to tell a story about what happens when the seed rots away. But the parable is not concerned with the fate of the grain, only with its productivity. The point is, Jesus had to die to bring life, just as we must die to our selfishness to find meaning and purpose in our lives.

While there is no similar parable in the other gospels, there is a passage in Paul's First Letter to the Corinthians that bears a striking resemblance. What Paul has to say in the fifteenth chapter of 1 Corinthians, brings to mind the parable from John. Speaking of the resurrection, Paul tells the church at Corinth: "But someone

---

1   Raymond Brown, *The Gospel of John I-XII*, New York: Doubleday 1966, p 472.

will ask, 'How are the dead raised? With what kind of body do they come?' Fool! What you sow does not come to life unless it dies. And as for what you sow, you do not sow the body that is to be, but a bare seed, perhaps of wheat or some other grain. But God gives it a body as he has chosen, and to each kind of seed its own body" (1 Cor. 15:35-38a).

What is Paul talking about? What is he trying to communicate to these first century Corinthians? Well, for example, think for a moment about all the lilies that decorate churches on Easter morning. Several months earlier, no one looking at the bulbs when they were planted could possibly have guessed that these bulbs would one day produce such magnificent blossoms. When you think about it, bulbs are rather ugly things. They are brown, shriveled up, altogether rather unattractive. But when planted and watered and cared for, they produce flowers more beautiful than we can ever adequately describe. Just looking at the bulb, no one would ever dream that all this was possible. But in a world where carpenters are resurrected, anything is possible.

So we sing:

"In the bulb there is a flower;
in the seed, an apple tree;
in cocoons, a hidden promise,
butterflies will soon be free!
In the cold and snow of winter,
there's a Spring that waits to be,
unrevealed until its season,
something God alone can see."[1]

During my forty-year ministry, I noticed several major changes in the way congregations decorate for Easter worship. More and more churches are using some kind of visual representation to try to capture the mystery of the resurrection. Many churches have taken to placing banners with images of butterflies on them throughout their sanctuaries. Just as with the bulb and the blossom of a lily, no one could possibly dream that such a beautiful thing as a Monarch

---

1   Words and Music: Natalie Sleeth 1986.

butterfly could come from such a lowly worm as the caterpillar. No wonder the early Christians chose the butterfly as the perfect symbol for Christ's resurrection. And no wonder that the practice is being returned to the church. Lilies and butterflies, with their bulbs and cocoons, point to a promise beyond themselves. Like a lily, one day we will bloom! Like a butterfly, we will emerge from our cocoon.

I don't think I have to remind you that we are talking about things that no one really knows anything about. But that does not mean that these things aren't true. The heart has reasons the mind has not yet begun to grasp.

Still, like the Corinthians, you may be asking much the same question. How is all this possible? I've seen a corpse, you say, and it pretty much looks like it's dead. All life, all animation, all force of energy is gone. How then shall we rise with this decaying body of ours?

Bear with me a moment. A little short course in the meaning of some of the words the Apostle Paul is using might turn out to be of help. The most helpful distinction is to realize that Paul had two words for body, not one. There is *sarx*, or flesh; and then there is *soma*, or body from which we get our word psychosomatic. The important thing is that neither Paul, nor any other New Testament writer for that matter, ever speaks of the resurrection of the flesh. But Paul does speak of the resurrection of the body.[1] Without a doubt, Paul felt a human being would need some kind of a body in the future life. He could not conceive otherwise. But that does not mean Paul expected this earthly flesh to make up that body. In Paul's way of thinking, *soma* is not the stuff that makes up the body; it is but the form of it. God will provide the stuff. As he says, "God will give it the body he chooses." In other verses Paul calls it a "glorified body." For us, that simply means that our resurrection into Christ will look more like the bloom of the lily than the bulb. But personally, I'm hoping for better hair than this baby fine, limp stuff covering most of my scalp! One thing we can count on is

1   *The Interpreters Dictionary of the Bible* Vol. R-Z, Buttrick, George, ed., New York: Abingdon Press 1962, p 52.

that we will have the body we need. It will be fitted for whatever life God has in store for us. Like Job we can say, "I know that my redeemer lives, and without my flesh I shall see God, who will be on my side, and not another." We will rise! What more do we need to know than that?

Well, maybe one more thing. Resurrection to new life is not just something that happens at the end of life, but throughout all of it. Every day of it, in fact.

There is a verse in the gospel of John that appears right in the middle of the story about Jesus' raising his good friend Lazarus from the dead. In this verse, we hear those magnificent words of hope that Jesus spoke to Lazarus' sister, Martha. "I am the resurrection and the life. Those who believe in me, even though they die, will live, and everyone who lives and believes in me will never die." Jesus says to Martha, "Do you believe this?" She said to him, "Yes, Lord, I believe that you are the Messiah, the Son of God, the one coming into the world."

But can't you just hear her add, "But would you please get down to the business of helping my brother? After all, he's been dead four days as it is!" Eventually, that's just what Jesus did. But Martha's worries are very much to the point. Don't we all hear ourselves saying, "This resurrection stuff is all well and good, but I can worry about the afterlife later. What I'm concerned about right now is how I'm going to get through the day." That's why it's such a comfort to learn that the resurrection is not just about what happened way back then, or what will happen later on, but what's going on right now.

Maybe it can be put this way: The difference between Jesus' raising Lazarus from the dead and Jesus himself being raised from the dead is that Lazarus was simply being resuscitated. Lazarus had to die all over again. Resurrection is not resuscitation; it's transformation. You see, Jesus' resurrection set loose a life-force in this world that can transform our lives right this very moment. It has the power to make us into the kind of sons and daughters God wants us to be. It can change us into the very likeness of Christ.

Resurrection is not just something that happens at the end of life, but all the way through it. Every day, in fact. Every day brings an opportunity to die to self and rise to newness of life. Each day, every day, we need to die to sin and rise to goodness. The same is true with those young boys and girls who on Easter morning in many churches are symbolically buried in the waters of Christian baptism and raised to new life in Christ. No, they will not need to be baptized over and over again. But they will need to remember, as we all do, what it means. There's a pattern to life, and it resembles the daily rhythm of rising and going to sleep, and rising again. It happens every time we forgive and are forgiven. It happens every time we get sick and then get well, or stand by someone who does. It happens every time we reach out to someone, or someone reaches out to us. It happens every time when we feel that we are alone and that no one cares, but then realize we do. It happens every time we don't know which way to turn, and then find a way where there was no way. It happens every time when we face death, or worse yet, the death of one we love, and then find that there is something stronger than death, love.

We will rise! In this life as well as the next. We can come to resemble a lily in this life as well as the next. We can fly like a butterfly right now. We don't even have to wait! For every day is Easter Day.

BIBLIOGRAPHY

Bass, Dorothy C. editor; *Practicing Our Faith*, San Francisco,CA: Josey Bass Publishers, 1997.

Brown, Raymond, *The Gospel of John I-XII*, New York: Doubleday, 1966.

Buttrick, George*, ed., The Interpreters Dictionary of the Bible Vol. R-Z*, New York: Abingdon Press 1962.

Davies, W.D., and Dale C. Allison Jr, *Matthew Vol. 2*, Edinburgh: T&T Clark, 1991.

Davies, W.D., and Dale C. Allison Jr., *Matthew Vol 3*, Edinburgh: T&T Clark 1991.

Harrelson, Walter J., General Editor, *The New Interpreter's ® Study Bible*, Abingdon Press, 2003.

Harrington, Daniel J., *The Gospel According to Matthew*, Collegeville Bible Commentary, Collegeville, Minnesota: The Liturgical Press, 1983.

Hooker, Morna, *The Gospel According to St. Mark*, London: Continum, 2001.

France, R.T., *Matthew*, Leicester, UK: Inter-Varsity Press, 1985.

France, R.T. *The Gospel of Mark*, Grand Rapids Michigan: Wm. B. Eerdmans Publishing Co., 2002.

McKenna, Megan, *The New Stations of the Cross*, USA: Doubleday, 2003.

Nouwen, Henri, *Sabbatical Journey*, London: Darton, Longman and Todd Ltd, 1998.

Patte, Daniel, *The Gospel According to Matthew*, Philadelphia, Pennsylvania: Fortress Press, 1987.

Peterson, Eugene H., *The Message*, Colorado Springs, CO: Navpress, 1993.

Wright, Tom, *Matthew for Everyone Part 1*, London: SPCK, 2002.

Wright, Tom, *Matthew for Everyone Part 2*, London: SPCK, 2002.

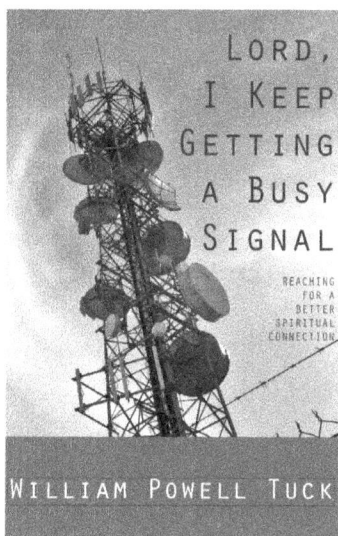

LORD,
I KEEP
GETTING
A BUSY
SIGNAL

REACHING
FOR A
BETTER
SPIRITUAL
CONNECTION

WILLIAM POWELL TUCK

Buy it, read it, and, above all, practice it. Your whole life will be different for having done so.

John Killinger
Former pastor, and professor at Vanderbilt, Chicago, Princeton and Samford University.

When Weiss walks you through the Gospel of John, the maze turns to amazement. You will discover another world with all the favorable conditions for a better life.

Abraham Terian
St. Nersess Armenian Seminary

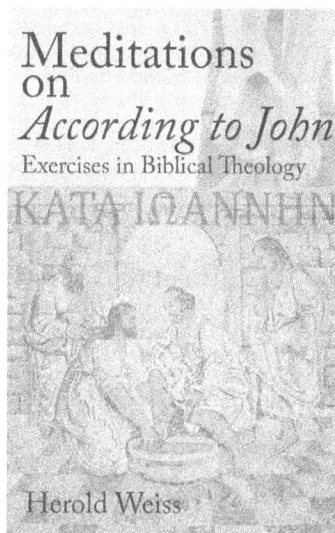

Meditations
on
According to John
Exercises in Biblical Theology
KATA IΩANNHN

Herold Weiss

MORE FROM ENERGION PUBLICATIONS

Personal Study

Holy Smoke! Unholy Fire	Bob McKibben	$14.99
The Jesus Paradigm	David Alan Black	$17.99
When People Speak for God	Henry Neufeld	$17.99
The Sacred Journey	Chris Surber	$11.99

Christian Living

It's All Greek to Me	David Alan Black	$3.99
Grief: Finding the Candle of Light	Jody Neufeld	$8.99
My Life Story	Becky Lynn Black	$14.99
Crossing the Street	Robert LaRochelle	$16.99
Life as Pilgrimage	David Moffett-Moore	14.99

Bible Study

Learning and Living Scripture	Lentz/Neufeld	$12.99
From Inspiration to Understanding	Edward W. H. Vick	$24.99
Philippians: A Participatory Study Guide	Bruce Epperly	$9.99
Ephesians: A Participatory Study Guide	Robert D. Cornwall	$9.99
Ecclesiastes: A Participatory Study Guide	Russell Meek	$9.99

Theology

Creation in Scripture	Herold Weiss	$12.99
Creation: the Christian Doctrine	Edward W. H. Vick	$12.99
The Politics of Witness	Allan R. Bevere	$9.99
Ultimate Allegiance	Robert D. Cornwall	$9.99
History and Christian Faith	Edward W. H. Vick	$9.99
The Journey to the Undiscovered Country	William Powell Tuck	$9.99
Process Theology	Bruce G. Epperly	$4.99

Ministry

Clergy Table Talk	Kent Ira Groff	$9.99
Out of This World	Darren McClellan	$24.99

Generous Quantity Discounts Available
Dealer Inquiries Welcome
Energion Publications — P.O. Box 841
Gonzalez, FL 32560
Website: http://energionpubs.com
Phone: (850) 525-3916

www.ingramcontent.com/pod-product-compliance
Lightning Source LLC
LaVergne TN
LVHW011207080426
835508LV00007B/655